Praise for *How to Eat Your Bible*

Any book that has as its goal to get people to more carefully read, faithfully understand, and joyfully treasure the Word of God is a gift I gratefully commend to the people of God. This message, so greatly needed in our day, cannot be heard too often or often enough.

NANCY DEMOSS WOLGEMUTH
Author, host/teacher of Revive Our Hearts

The spirit of J. C. Ryle pulses through this short yet arresting book. In an age that urges us to be justified by doubt, not by faith, Pickowicz does something unusual: he counsels us to eat the words of God like food. In doing so, he models a deep love for and trust in Scripture. The result is a readable book that is as catalytic as it is instructive. What a gift! We learn here that the Bible is not for super-scholars, or far-out mystical gurus, or shiny-toothed salesmen. The Bible is for me, and in it I will meet God, and by it, I will see Him face-to-face.

OWEN STRACHAN
Author of *Reenchanting Humanity: A Theology of Mankind*; associate professor of Christian theology, Midwestern Baptist Theological Seminary

In this book, Nate shares how God enabled him to go from a person who read the Bible "from time to time" to someone who cannot have enough of this life-transforming book. Yet this is not only a testimony; it is also a brief educational tour in how you too can find yourself delighting in an intellectually stretching and spiritually satisfying daily reading of Scripture. Are you becoming lethargic in your regular intake of God's Word? Read this practical book and it will propel you to a fresh love for the good old book!

CONRAD MBEWE
Pastor of Kabwata Baptist Church, Lusaka, Zambia

How to Eat Your Bible is for every Christian. Whether you're a seasoned theologian, a new believer, a young person struggling with doubts, or a pastor firm in your faith, this book will improve your understanding of and ability to teach Scripture. *How to Eat Your Bible* shows a world starving for truth how to "taste and see that the Lord is good" by studying His Word.

Al̲l̲i̲e̲ ̲B̲

1
(

You're Not Enough (And That's

So many miss the thrill of knowing God through His Word because they simply don't know what to do with the Bible. You may read the Bible, but you don't know how to eat the Bible. Nate Pickowicz sets the table for the hungry soul in *How to Eat Your Bible*. Simple, practical, and profoundly biblical, this book serves as a menu to guide those hungering for more— more of God, more of Christ, and more of Scripture. Learn how to read, study, and eat more than you ever have. The feast has been prepared, sit down at the table and enjoy!

DUSTIN W. BENGE
Provost, Union School of Theology, Bridgend, Wales

If you struggle with reading your Bible, if you can't seem to figure out a consistent way to get in God's Word, let *How to Eat Your Bible* intensify your hunger for the Scriptures. This short book will help you with both the why and the how of consuming God's Word, guiding you to the transforming, satisfying, sufficient truth found within the pages of the Book.

ABIGAIL DODDS
Author of *(A) Typical Woman: Free, Whole, and Called in Christ*

One of the greatest threats facing Christianity is Christians who do not know the Word of God. It is only when we know the unchanging Word of God in a constantly changing world that we will turn the world upside down by the power of the Holy Spirit and the preaching of the gospel. This book helps to lay the foundation for knowing God's Word, loving God's Word, and being doers of God's Word as we rest in the power of God's Word. I am grateful for this clear and accessible book for the church of Jesus Christ.

BURK PARSONS
Senior Pastor of Saint Andrew's Chapel and editor of *Tabletalk* magazine

HOW
TO
EAT
YOUR
BIBLE

*A Simple Approach to Learning
and Loving the Word of God*

Nate Pickowicz

MOODY PUBLISHERS

CHICAGO

THE MASTER'S SEMINARY PRESS

LOS ANGELES

© 2021 by
NATE PICKOWICZ

All rights reserved. No part of this book may be reproduced in any form without permission in writing from the publisher, except in the case of brief quotations embodied in critical articles or reviews.

All Scripture quotations, unless otherwise indicated, are taken from the New American Standard Bible®, copyright © 1960, 1962, 1963, 1968, 1971, 1972, 1973, 1975, 1977, 1995 by The Lockman Foundation. Used by permission. (www.Lockman.org)

Edited by Kevin P. Emmert
Interior Design: Kaylee Lockenour
Cover Design: Darren Welch Design
Cover photo of Bible copyright © 2017 by arKsteer / iStock (891692100).
Cover photo of plate copyright © 2019 by New Africa / Shutterstock (1422010598).
Cover photo of knife and fork copyright © 2019 by nevodka / iStock (112225148).
All rights reserved for all of the above photos.
Author Photo: Carla Howe

All websites and phone numbers listed herein are accurate at the time of publication but may change in the future or cease to exist. The listing of website references and resources does not imply publisher endorsement of the site's entire contents. Groups and organizations are listed for informational purposes, and listing does not imply publisher endorsement of their activities.

Library of Congress Cataloging-in-Publication Data

Names: Pickowicz, Nate, author.
Title: How to eat your Bible : a simple approach to learning and loving the
   word of God / Nate Pickowicz.
Description: Chicago : Moody Publishers ; Los Angeles : The Master's
   Seminary Press, 2021. | Includes bibliographical references. | Summary:
   "How to Eat Your Bible offers an entry point into Scripture that will
   help you cultivate an appetite for life-long study of God's Word. Find
   practical guidance for overcoming the hurdles that have kept you from
   making Bible study a regular part of your life"-- Provided by publisher.
Identifiers: LCCN 2020034632 (print) | LCCN 2020034633 (ebook) | ISBN
   9780802420398 (paperback) | ISBN 9780802498960 (ebook)
Subjects: LCSH: Bible--Appreciation. | Bible--Criticism, interpretation,
   etc.
Classification: LCC BS538 .P53 2020 (print) | LCC BS538 (ebook) | DDC
   220.071--dc23
LC record available at https://lccn.loc.gov/2020034632
LC ebook record available at https://lccn.loc.gov/2020034633

Originally delivered by fleets of horse-drawn wagons, the affordable paperbacks from D. L. Moody's publishing house resourced the church and served everyday people. Now, after more than 125 years of publishing and ministry, Moody Publishers' mission remains the same— even if our delivery systems have changed a bit. For more information on other books (and resources) created from a biblical perspective, go to www.moodypublishers.com or write to:

Moody Publishers
820 N. LaSalle Boulevard
Chicago, IL 60610

5 7 9 10 8 6 4

Printed in the United States of America

To my children

CONTENTS

CONTENTS

FOREWORD

Like so many good "church kids," I grew up hearing about the importance of personal devotions—of a daily time of reading the Bible and praying. But, like so many good "church kids," I built the habit carelessly and casually, more to assuage my guilt and mollify my parents than to actually study the Word and to relate to the God of the Word. To be honest, it wasn't until I had moved out and was married, until I had independence and responsibilities, that I began to know my need for such disciplines and, therefore, until I began to prioritize them in my life. Today I can't imagine my life (and frankly, don't wish to imagine my life) without a daily time with the Lord.

Along the way, my experience was similar to Nate Pickowicz's in that I encountered John MacArthur's Bible-reading plan—a plan that involves repeated readings of a single book until that book is firmly fixed in the mind and heart. This became very meaningful and very helpful to me. Yet while I found this plan helpful, and a means to read the Bible both deeply and widely, I eventually modified it. After all, just as there are many ways to read the Bible badly, there are many ways to read the Bible fruitfully.

What I so appreciate about *How To Eat Your Bible* is not only that Pickowicz provides a plan to help you read your Bible consistently and well, but that he provides that plan only after he offers a basic theology of Scripture and Scripture-reading. Long before he offers one man's method of reading the Bible, he explains the value of following *some* method of reading the Bible (even if it is not his). Then, for those who are looking for a plan, or eager to try a new one, he offers his Seven Year Bible Plan, which, if followed, will necessarily both deepen and widen your knowledge of the Word of God and, therefore, your knowledge of God Himself. And what could be more important than that?

Tim Challies
Author of *Do More Better*
Blogger at Challies.com

SETTING THE TABLE

'm writing this book to myself. Well, actually, it's for you, but I can't help wondering whether you and I may have had a similar experience. I vividly remember a point in my life when the Bible was completely foreign to me. I had heard and understood the gospel, confessed my sins to the Lord, believed in Jesus Christ alone for salvation, attended church regularly, given financially, served joyfully, prayed often, participated in small groups, told other people about Jesus, and even played in the praise band. But amid it all, I knew something big was lacking in my Christian life. I didn't read my Bible.

It wasn't that I *never* read my Bible. I spot-read every now and then, I jotted down verses and put them on my fridge, I listened to inspiring sermons on Christian radio, and I even memorized a few key verses. Having grown up going to church, I had a small arsenal of about twenty to thirty verses that I knew by heart, and I would trot them out in Christian circles so as not to appear completely ignorant or unspiritual.

But when I was being honest with myself, I really didn't *know* the Bible. For me, the New Testament felt daunting, and the Old Testament felt like a foreign language. At one point, I distinctly remember lumbering my way through a Bible reading plan, which I finished with relief, but I could barely remember what I had read or why it mattered.

My lack of Bible knowledge or spiritual understanding had become a source of embarrassment and shame. At one point in my young adult life, I worked for a Christian businessman who often tried to encourage me with the Scriptures. However, when he began to notice inconsistencies in my Christian walk, he called me into his office one day and began to press me on my spiritual disciplines. He asked me, "Are you reading your Bible?" *Oh no, he's on to me!* I thought. I gave a somewhat-rehearsed answer, "Well, you know, I miss a day or two here and there." But he was no dummy. "What's your favorite Bible verse?" he asked. Well, I had a handful of canned verses tucked away in my mind from Awana when I was eight years old. I gave him one of those. *Phew!* It seemed to work—for the time being.

But I didn't want to spend my whole life dodging Bible questions and faking my commitment to Scripture. Furthermore, when I was being honest with myself, I knew full well that even if I was able to fool other people, I couldn't fool God. If I knew anything at all from Sunday school lessons as a kid, it was that God knew my heart, and I wasn't able to hide from Him.

And so, I had no choice but to confess: *I didn't love the Word of God.*

More than that, *I didn't even know the Word of God.*

Sadly, I wasn't the only one.

So what is the solution? How do we fight our biblical illiteracy? As we'll see a little later in the book, I think the problem is multifaceted. But at the core of the problem, I believe, is a lack of conviction of the Bible's power and ability to change us and make us more like Christ.

Let's talk about this.

IS THE BIBLE ENOUGH?

During the sixteenth century in Europe, the Protestant Reformers fought a battle for the heart of Christianity. One of the key issues they contended for was that of authority. Who has the right to tell Christians what to do? The Roman Catholic Church claimed that the Church itself, according to Scripture and tradition, had supreme spiritual authority over all people. But the Reformers insisted on *sola Scriptura*—"Scripture alone"—as our chief, supreme, and ultimate authority.[1] This was nothing short of a battle over the authority and sufficiency of the Word of God.

In dealing with the issue of sufficiency, it's helpful to look at 2 Timothy 3:16, a key text in understanding the doctrine of Scripture. Not only does Paul declare, "All Scripture is inspired by God," but he adds four modifiers, namely that Scripture is "profitable for teaching, for reproof, for correction, for training in righteousness." Let's look at these.

First, he says that Scripture is profitable for *teaching*. This is instructive teaching for how every Christian is to think, believe, and live. How do we know what God desires for us to believe about the world, humanity, Jesus Christ, the gospel, government, the church, marriage, family, work, speech, leisure, and so on? The Bible instructs every believer on all matters of life and faith.

Next, Scripture is profitable for *reproof*. This has to do with rebuke that is designed to bring about repentance and a change of thinking or action. Often, we operate with wrong or misguided beliefs about our lives. Sometimes these beliefs are shaped by our sinful hearts; other times they're produced out of sheer ignorance. Whatever the cause may be, the Bible seeks to attack our wrong presuppositions, exposing them for what they are. To use a biblical metaphor, the Bible shines a light into dark places in order to expose the things that are hidden (Eph. 5:13).

Scripture is also profitable for *correction*, which is the flip side of reproof—a positive exhortation, not just away from wrongdoing but toward doing what is right according to God's standard. It's one thing to discipline a rebellious child for doing the wrong thing, but nothing will ever change without further correcting them toward doing the right thing. The Bible does both.

Lastly, Scripture is profitable for *training in righteousness*. This is the application of biblical truth, the obedience of faith (Rom. 1:5). Jesus told His followers in the Great Commission of Matthew 28:19–20 that they should be teaching disciples to obey all that He had commanded. So much of the Bible (especially the New Testament) is instructive. Whether through direct instruction or through examination of the lives of persons, we are trained by God through His words to conform to His righteous standard.

What is the ultimate practical purpose? Paul continues in 2 Timothy 3:17, "so that the man of God may be adequate, equipped for every good work." The goal of reading, studying, and applying the Scripture is that the believer would be built up, equipped, and matured for every good work that God has prepared for them to do (Eph. 2:10). In other words, Scripture is sufficient to minister to every aspect of your life. The Word of God can change you. But how?

HOW THE BIBLE CHANGES YOU

In Matthew 4, when Satan tempted Jesus in the wilderness, Jesus fired back by saying, "Man shall not live on bread alone, but on every word that proceeds out of the mouth of God" (v. 4). What did He mean? Jesus was pointing to the soul-transforming, soul-satisfying Word (more on that later). All the pleasures of the world can provide only partial and temporary comfort, but the Word of God regenerates, illuminates, ingratiates, and motivates. Let's look briefly at a few ways the Scriptures can change and satisfy you.

It Changes Your Spirit (Regeneration)

The Bible makes the exclusive claim to be the means by which people are saved through the message of the gospel.

We read, "Faith comes from hearing, and hearing by the word of Christ" (Rom. 10:17). We understand that we aren't saved by doing works but by hearing and believing the gospel by faith (Gal. 3:2). But, what is the gospel? The gospel is the good news regarding the death, burial, and resurrection of Jesus Christ. The good news is that, because of the sacrificial work of Jesus, we can be forgiven of our sins, reconciled to God, and ushered into the kingdom of heaven.

Ephesians 1:13 affirms to us that, "after listening to [or reading!] the message of truth, the gospel of [our] salvation—having also believed, [we are] sealed . . . with the Holy Spirit of promise." The Spirit regenerates our souls; we are "born again" (John 3:3–8), given a brand-new life in Jesus Christ. The message of the gospel in the Scriptures carries with it the power to give new spiritual life to those who believe (Rom. 1:16). For a person who has not yet been saved, reading the Bible can bring them from death to life through the gospel of Jesus Christ.

It Changes Your Mind (Knowledge)

According to Proverbs 2:6, "The LORD gives wisdom; from His mouth come knowledge and understanding." The Bible is clear that true knowledge comes from God. The apostle Paul prayed that the believers in Colossae would "be filled with the knowledge of [God's] will in all spiritual wisdom and understanding" (Col. 1:9). In short, the Lord desires us to know Him, and studying the Bible is the primary way we come to know Him.

Further, the Word of God not only provides knowledge and wisdom, but also has the power to renew and change your mind (Rom. 12:1–2). In studying the Bible, we learn to think God's thoughts after Him. In other words, we learn to think in *biblical categories*. Even the most childlike believer can read the Bible and receive wisdom and understanding from the Lord (Ps. 119:130). And while our sinful minds will ultimately be set on trivial and evil things, a biblically informed, Spirit-filled mind will set itself on life and peace (Rom. 8:6).

Do you want a changed mind, a mind that is renewed by the things of God?

Read your Bible.

It Changes Your Emotions (Affections)

The Word of God can not only regenerate your soul and alter the way you think, but can also change the way you feel. We are emotional creatures, and while we don't want to be beholden to our emotions, a growing relationship with God will certainly affect the way we feel. One of the most common expressions of emotion tied to the knowledge of God is *joy*. David exclaimed, "O how I love Your law! It is my meditation all the day" (Ps. 119:97). Jeremiah declared, "Your words were found and I ate them, and Your words became for me a joy and the delight of my heart" (Jer. 15:16). After learning the Scriptures from Jesus on the road to Emmaus, the two disciples said to one another, "Were not our hearts burning within us while He was speaking to us on the road, while He was explaining the Scriptures to us?" (Luke 24:32).

Of course, learning the Bible can also produce feelings of *sorrow*, especially over sinfulness. We read in Hebrews 4:12 that "the word of God is living and active and sharper than any two-edged sword, and piercing as far as the division of soul and spirit, of both joints and marrow, and able to judge the thoughts and intentions of the heart." When this happens and sin is exposed, the Word produces godly grief. For example, when the unbelieving crowd heard the gospel in Peter's sermon, Acts 2:37 says that "they were pierced to the heart"—they were sorrowful and longed for forgiveness. Studying the Bible should produce no less in us. But the changes shouldn't stop at our emotions.

It Changes Your Will (Volition)

Once we have received new life in Jesus Christ, have had our minds enlightened to the things of God, and have been affected emotionally, we are compelled to act. The Bible exhorts Christians toward godly action. The Lord desires us to become conformed to Christ's image (Rom. 8:29). We are to be *sanctified*. In fact, Jesus prayed to the Father that He would "sanctify them in the truth; Your word is truth" (John 17:17). What does it mean to be sanctified? It means we are cleansed spiritually, presented to Christ as holy, set apart, and made blameless before Him (Eph. 5:26–27). In other words, our lives should be changed by what we know about God.

In fact, Paul tells us that having our minds renewed by

God's Word produces a lifestyle of worship (Rom. 12:1–2). We think, talk, and act in ways that bear spiritual fruit and therefore please God (Col. 1:10). We aren't just meant to *know* the right answers about God; He desires us to obey Him with our lives. Jesus said, "If you love Me, you will keep My commandments" (John 14:15). Knowing the Bible should ultimately lead us to a greater obedience to the Lord in all things.

In short, the Bible is powerful and able to change your life from the inside out. No other means is given by God to accomplish such a task. The Spirit of God, who is at work in the hearts of Christians, uses the Word of God to transform them into Christlike people. And so, to neglect the discipline of Bible reading and study is to cut off the very source of spiritual food that you need to live a Christian life. But if you're like me and have experienced the frustration of not knowing *how* or *where* to begin, I pray that this book encourages and instructs you.

Now, if you realize that you're not a Christian, then I'm *really* glad you picked up this book! It's my greatest hope that you would see your need for the Savior, turn from your sins, and trust in Jesus Christ today. Nothing in the world is more important than that!

But if you *are* a Christian, yet you're struggling to read and understand your Bible, this book was written for you. It's a book about how to not just read but truly feast on Scripture. My hope is that you would learn how to eat your Bible.

Summary: The Word of God is *sufficient* to minister to every part of our condition and has the power to transform us in all the way of godliness. Furthermore, it has the power to change your spirit, mind, emotions, and will.

CHAPTER ONE

STARVING FOR THE WORD

If you were to open your Bible to the exact middle point, you would land in Psalm 119. Written by King David a thousand years before the time of Jesus, Psalm 119 is the longest single passage in Scripture, glorying in the wonder and splendor of the Word of God. When you read the psalm, you cannot escape the conclusion that David *loves* the Word of God. He speaks of it with such tender affection and deep longing. He pens lines like, "Your word I have treasured in my heart" (v. 11), "I have rejoiced in the way of Your testimonies" (v. 14), "Your testimonies . . . are my delight" (v. 24), "I shall delight in Your commandments, which I love" (v. 47), "O how I love Your law!" (v. 97), "How sweet are Your words to my taste! Yes, sweeter than honey to my mouth!" (v. 103), "Your testimonies are wonderful" (v. 129), "I rejoice at Your word, as one who finds great spoil" (v. 162), "Your law is my delight" (v. 174). Verse after verse, David continues to praise the Lord and declares his love for God's Word.

It could easily be a struggle to identify with David's sentiments. Even if we are able to read the Bible, we may not be as eager to confess such affection for it. *Don't you think you're taking this a little too far, David? I mean, after all, it's just a book, right?* But when you read all 176 verses of Psalm 119, one thing becomes very clear: God desires believers to know and love His Word.

But this has been a constant human struggle for ages.

FAMINE IN THE LAND

The people of God were prospering under King Jeroboam II during the eighth century BC, but not all was well in Israel. Despite the fact that God had blessed the nation with wealth and political dominance, the Israelites were living in open rebellion to the Lord and violating His commands. After many warnings, God sent the prophet Amos to rebuke them and deliver a message of coming judgment. Unbeknownst to Israel, their destruction was not far away. The Assyrians invaded in the year 722 BC, and carried off the bulk of Israel into captivity. However, prior to their fall, Amos prophesied a far worse judgment than captivity:

> "Behold, days are coming," declares the
>   Lord GOD,
> "When I will send a famine on the land,
> Not a famine for bread or a thirst for
>   water,

*But rather for hearing the words of the
     LORD.
"People will stagger from sea to sea
And from the north even to the east;
They will go to and fro to seek the word
     of the LORD,
But they will not find it." (Amos 8:11–12)*

What Amos describes is a horrible time when the people of God, longing to hear a word from the Lord, will be unable to due to His prescribed spiritual famine. In the earlier years, when they had easy access to the Scriptures, they were sluggish and indifferent to the things of God. It would be another two hundred years before they would be restored to where they were before the judgment.

When we examine this point in Israel's history, it's not difficult to see parallels that can be made of our modern age. For example, America is a financially prosperous, politically powerful nation that is feared and respected worldwide. However, we are arguably one of the most morally loose and spiritually bankrupt nations as well. And while there may be several key factors that contribute to it, our modern biblical illiteracy epidemic no doubt has a part to play. And while it's possible to know the Word of God and be morally bankrupt, the problem of biblical illiteracy feels very much like a judgment of God because of our national sinfulness.

The Bible Illiteracy Epidemic

In the years following the Protestant Reformation in Europe, for the first time in a millennium, the Bible had become accessible to a large number of Christians. With the invention of the Gutenberg printing press, Bibles were being mass-produced in numerous languages and being sent around the world. This amazing advancement created opportunities for even the youngest and poorest believers to have access to the Scriptures. A popular English translation was made in Geneva in 1560, which was readily used by the Puritans and even the Pilgrims that sailed across the Atlantic Ocean. Later, in the next century, King James I commissioned the translation of the Bible, called the *Authorized Version*, which has been used by scores of believers all throughout the English-speaking world over the last four hundred years.

The twentieth century alone produced more Bible translations than perhaps any other time in human history, which included the American Standard Version (ASV), the Revised Standard Version (RSV), the New American Standard Bible (NASB), the New International Version (NIV), and the English Standard Version (ESV, released just after the turn of the century)—to name just a few. We have more access to Scripture than at any other point in human history. A 2014 study found that 88 percent of Americans own a Bible.[1] More than this, it's estimated that the average family has 4.7 Bibles in their home.[2] And with the invention of the iPhone, virtually every person on the planet has access to the

Bible electronically. In fact, even if every physical Bible was destroyed, it would be nearly impossible to erase the digital witness of Scripture on the internet.

However, despite having unfettered access to the Bible in our modern age, it seems as though our appetite for the Word of God is greatly diminished. In fact, a more recent survey revealed that 48 percent of American adults are completely disengaged from Bible reading, with another 9 percent reporting that they interact with Scripture sporadically.[3] This shows us that the Bible has little to no impact on the lives of nearly 6 out of 10 people. Seizing on this problem, there have been countless books, articles, and blog posts about the problems of biblical illiteracy over the last decade.[4] In fact, one researcher has confessed his belief that biblical literacy has reached "a crisis point," even describing the problem as a *famine*. New Testament scholar Kenneth Berding writes, "Christians used to be known as 'people of one book,'" adding that "They memorized it, meditated on it, talked about it and taught it to others." He continues, "We don't do that anymore, and in a very real sense we're starving ourselves to death."[5]

But why is this happening? There may be several key reasons, such as postmodernism's distrust of religion, self-reliance, social media distractions, entertainment, and addiction to busyness. Whatever the reason, it's hard not to think that we're living in a time similar to a biblically prosperous Israel just prior to the judgments of Amos.

Our problem is not that we do not have access to the Bible, or that God is deliberately withholding His special revelation from us. More than any other time in human history, His Word is sitting at our fingertips. All we have to do is pick it up. Learning to love God's Word is not just possible, it's doable. And history is full of believers whose love for God manifested itself in their love for His Word.

LEARNING TO LOVE THE WORD OF GOD

The life of an Old Testament prophet was pretty miserable. Prophesying during the time of spiritual famine, Jeremiah and Ezekiel were marked by hardship and sadness. In the face of turmoil, however, the revelation of God became their sole source of comfort, strength, and joy.

The prophet Jeremiah spent his entire life battling with stiff-necked and hardened people. In fact, his ministry became so disheartening that he mourned the fact that he had even been born. However, in the midst of his sadness, Jeremiah took comfort in the Lord's ministry *to him*—the ministry of the Word of God:

> *Your words were found and I ate them,*
> *And Your words became for me a joy*
> *and the delight of my heart;*
> *For I have been called by Your name,*
> *O LORD God of hosts. (Jer. 15:16)*

Despite his despair and utter depression over the state of his own country, he had learned to love the Word of God and take great comfort in it, confessing that Scripture had become "a joy" and a "delight" to him. Regardless of what

26

was happening around him, his spiritual appetite was satiated by devouring God's Word.

Ezekiel had a companion ministry to that of Jeremiah: Jeremiah was prophesying in the spiritual wasteland in Jerusalem while Ezekiel ministered to the exiles in Babylon. The primary job of a prophet was to speak God's word to God's people. In order to accomplish this calling, the prophet needed to know the word so intimately that it was seeping through his pores. Ezekiel reflects upon the time the Lord called him:

> Then He said to me, "Son of man, eat what you find; eat this scroll, and go, speak to the house of Israel." So I opened my mouth, and He fed me this scroll. He said to me, "Son of man, feed your stomach and fill your body with this scroll which I am giving you." Then I ate it, and it was sweet as honey in my mouth.
> . . . Moreover, He said to me, "Son of man, take into your heart all My words which I will speak to you and listen closely." (Ezek. 3:1–3, 10)

While we know that God doesn't literally shove pieces of parchment into Ezekiel's mouth, Ezekiel describes vividly the act of receiving the Scriptures from the Lord and ingesting their content so intimately that he can describe the act only as *eating*. What was his response to such an intense experience with the Word of God? He describes their effect as being "sweet as honey in my mouth" (v. 3). This is not unlike David's experience with Scripture, declaring, "How sweet are Your words to my taste! Yes, sweeter than honey to my mouth!" (Ps. 119:103).

I find it hard to read verses like these and not stand amazed at the testimonies of people like David, Ezekiel, and Jeremiah—those who devour Scripture and delight so richly in it. It makes me wonder whether our current approaches to the Word of God are geared toward helping us learn to love it so. Are we truly being trained and encouraged to love God's Word, or are we falling into the trap of becoming, as David Nienhuis warns, "merely informed quoters of the Word"—those who are prone "to memorize a select set of Bible verses" over helping believers become truly transformed by the Word?[6] While memorizing Bible verses should no doubt become part of our study (as we'll see later), our real focus should be on developing a long-term understanding and love for the Bible.

Keeping the Long View

For years, one of the more popular approaches to daily devotions has been built on reading through the whole Bible once a year. To be clear, there's nothing wrong with reading through the Bible once a year consistently, but we're living in unprecedented times. We simply do not have the luxury of assuming that most modern-day believers have the baseline of Bible knowledge that their parents or grandparents had. Generally speaking, churches are doing less and less Bible teaching, few parents catechize their children, and culture is overwhelmingly Scripture averse. I recently heard the story of a Sunday school teacher who asked her class if anyone knew what Palm Sunday was. To her dismay, after a few awkward moments, one child raised his hand, spread his fingers and pointed to his palm. He wasn't joking.

And so, we're simply not exposed to the Bible. More than this, as Christians, we generally feel ashamed about it. So what do we do?

Without kicking anyone's reading plans to the curb, I'm suggesting that we alter our focus a bit. Because here's how it generally goes: Like other New Year's resolutions, you start your reading plan in January with the best of intentions, and as you work through Genesis and Exodus, you're sailing! Then you hit Leviticus and start to lose some steam, but you press on. A few jaunts in the genealogies of Chronicles and you're starting to question yourself: *Why isn't this interesting to me? Did I miss something?* Whereas many people seem to fall off around the Major Prophets (Isaiah, Jeremiah, Ezekiel, and Daniel), you grit your teeth and power through, eyes skimming over whole paragraphs of content. A late summer cold and a throbbing sinus headache make it impossible to read, so you lose half the Minor Prophets. By the time you get to Jesus in the Gospels, you've forgotten nearly everything from the Old Testament, but you're relieved to finally be in the New Testament. The stories and parables are sweetly familiar, and the missionary journeys of Acts are exciting. But then you hit nineteen letters of doctrine, followed by the head-scratching symbolism of Revelation. And while all your church friends fell off their reading plans months ago,[7] at least you finished—but you retained so little that you secretly wonder why you even attempted it in the first place.

This may not resemble your experience, but I've talked to countless Christians who have made such confessions to me. Now, if "Bible-in-a-Year" is working for you, no one is telling you to stop. But I'm guessing that you didn't pick up this book because you feel like you're knocking it out of the park.

So let me encourage you.

Instead of plowing through a few verses and then speeding off to work, slow it down. Instead of laboring through the whole Bible in a year, go a little deeper. Instead of reading your Bible simply to check it off the chore list, change your mental approach—change your philosophy.[8] Instead, take a longer view of learning your Bible—two, three, five, or even seven years. Make your end goal not merely to read the Bible but to know and understand it—to *love* and *treasure* it as God's holy, sufficient, transforming Word.

I distinctly remember being in a place of utter desperation and needing some fresh air. It was at that place that I discovered this paradigm shift.

REDISCOVERING THE BIBLE

As I sat there with my head in my hands, the workday was half gone, but I couldn't even think about my job. I felt lost and alone, depressed and dejected. Like watching a car wreck in slow motion, I knew my life had been veering off course into spiritual ruin. Why did I still feel distant from God? I was desperate for a sign, for an affirmation, for a word from heaven. What did God want from me? What did He want me to do? I had no idea. But deep down, I knew there was one thing wrong—something I was still neglecting. I reasoned, "I do everything else I'm supposed to do. He can't really be *that* upset that I don't read my Bible, can He?" I tried every excuse I could think of, but in the end, I knew that I was being disobedient.

A few years earlier, my father had given me a study Bible, which sat on the shelf in my office. While there wasn't a sign above it that read, "Break Glass and Use in the Event of an Emergency," I had treated the Bible that way. But that day felt like an emergency. So I grabbed it and thumped it onto my desk. When I *did* read my Bible, my method usually consisted of skimming through the pages until a verse jumped out at me. That, after all, is surely a sign that God wants to you read it, right? So I began to thumb through. Nothing. In a last-ditch effort, I turned to the front of the Bible and read the introduction. It would change my life forever.

The Seven Year Bible Plan

In God's providence, the Bible my dad had given me was *The MacArthur Study Bible*, and in the introduction, there is a section titled, "How to Study the Bible." I thought, *Well, if anybody knows how to study the Bible, it must be this MacArthur guy.* So I read.

31

Read through the Old Testament at least once a year. As you read, note in the margins any truths you particularly want to remember, and write down separately anything you do not immediately understand. Often as you read you will find that many questions are answered by the text itself. The questions to which you cannot find answers become the starting points for more in-depth study using commentaries or other reference tools.

Follow a different plan for reading the New Testament. Read one book at a time repetitiously for a month or more. This will help to retain what is in the New Testament and not always have to depend on a concordance to find things.

If you want to try this, begin with a short book, such as 1 John, and read it through in one sitting every day for 30 days. At the end of that time, you will know what is in the book. Write on index cards the major theme of each chapter. By referring to the cards as you do your daily reading, you will begin to remember the content of each chapter. In fact, you will develop a visual perception of the book in your mind.

Divide longer books into short sections and read each section daily for 30 days. For example, the gospel of

*John contains 21 chapters. Divide it into
3 sections of 7 chapters. At the end of
90 days, you will finish John. For variety,
alternate short and long books, and in
less than 3 years you will have finished
the entire New Testament—and you will
really know it!*[9]

Suddenly, my whole world opened up. Up to that point,
the thought of reading and understanding the Bible had
seemed daunting. But now, for the first time, I had hope!
After all, I had tried reading the whole Bible in a year and
failed many times, but studying the Bible book by book
seemed possible.

Days stretched into weeks, which stretched into months.
Chapter after chapter, book after book—I was actually
reading and studying the Bible! With each new section, my
understanding continued to grow. Before I knew it, I had
finished the whole New Testament, having read it thirty
times. And while I didn't feel like I had any sort of mastery
of the text, I identified with the sentiment uttered by Martin
Luther: "If you picture the Bible to be a mighty tree and every
word a little branch, I have shaken every one of these branches
because I wanted to know what it was and what it meant."[10]

As I continued on to the Old Testament, I began to share
my findings with others. As I began to talk with friends and
church people about Bible reading, they began to convey
their struggles. Very quickly, it became apparent that help
was needed, and I wanted to create a duplicable plan that I
could share with others. While I very openly shared that my

inspiration came from *The MacArthur Study Bible*, I had made some drastic modifications to the plan, including a more comprehensive approach to studying the Old Testament. Within a few years, I had developed "The Seven Year Bible Plan." This plan will be discussed at the end of the book.

Fundamentally, the plan is built on the MacArthur reading plan. The basic idea is: *read each book of the New Testament thirty times over three years.* However, I soon found myself desiring to alter my approach. At the beginning, I stayed pretty close to the MacArthur plan, but I began tweaking it slightly. Instead of logging the number of *days* in a book, I started tracking the number of "reads" through the book. By doing multiple daily readings, I was able to cover more ground in a shorter time, yet hopefully without sacrificing the needed time to study and meditate on the text. After completing the New Testament in three years, I altered the reading method and applied it to the Old Testament, shortening the number of "reads" down to fifteen. This allowed me to complete the Old Testament in just over four years.

> *New Testament: 30x through each book*
> *= approximately 3 years*
> *Old Testament: 15x through each book*
> *= approximately 4 years*

My aim for this book is far more than simply giving you this reading plan; my aim is ultimately to help you develop a long-term approach to lasting Bible study. As we proceed in our discussion, I'm going to offer study helps and exhortations designed to encourage you wherever you are, and using whatever plan with which you are most comfortable. For me, the Seven Year Bible Plan was transformational, but it is by no means the only way to learn and love the Scriptures. I'm convinced that our focus needs to be building lasting, sustainable habits and disciplines. Every newborn must learn how to eat in order to stay alive for a lifetime. As spiritually reborn people, we must also learn how to eat spiritual food (1 Peter 2:1–3) in order to endure until we are called home to be with the Lord. Therefore, we must learn to eat our Bibles.

ERRORS TO AVOID

As we're learning how to "eat our Bibles," we want to be careful not to get indigestion! Therefore, I want to offer a word of caution. In learning to love God's Word, there are two errors we ought to avoid:

First, *don't become prideful.* If you were to take every sin listed in the Bible and rank them according to God's hatred of it, pride would be at the very top (see Prov. 6:16–17). God opposes pride at every twist and turn. He can't stand it. So if you find yourself growing in your Bible knowledge and love for the Scriptures, guard yourself against pride. I always cringe a little when I see Christians posting pictures of their marked-up, highlighted, dilapidated Bibles on social media. Now, to be clear, there's something beautiful about seeing the fruit of years of intimate Bible study. Charles Spurgeon famously said, "A Bible that's falling apart usually belongs to someone who isn't." There's some wisdom to that. Read your Bible, study it, learn it, know it. Just don't brag about it to everyone around you. Don't go out of your way to show others how much you read, or how full the margins are with illegible chicken-scratch, or how many times you've had your Bible rebound. To put some mild spin on Jesus' maxim in Matthew 6:3, when you read your Bible, do not let your left hand know what your right hand is doing. Avoid pride at all costs.

Second, *don't be ashamed.* There are many reasons why Christians don't read their Bibles, but guilt and shame usually play a huge part in keeping them from growing in this area. Most Christians know they *should* be reading the Bible but struggle to have the desire or the practical know-how to do so effectively. As they grow more and more frustrated over this, their guilty conscience begins to weigh them down, and they become depressed. And the longer it persists, even the sight of the two-inch thick study Bible sitting on their nightstand causes the pit in their stomach to sink even deeper until they finally retire the book to the shelf, convinced that "maybe I'm just not a reader."

Let me encourage you: *God desires for you to know and love His Word.* Of all the possible things you would chase in this life that God could be against, Bible study isn't one of them. In fact, He's prepared to strive *with* you to help you. Prepare your heart, stay humble, and be encouraged! Cast off all your guilt and shame, and lift your eyes up to Christ. And as we work our way through this book, my prayer for you is that your heart would ignite for the Lord, that your desire for His Word would consume your waking thoughts, and that your love for Christ would abound in all joy and thanksgiving.

But before we dive into the Bible, we need to ask for help.

Summary: Despite having easy access to the Bible, our current American culture suffers from severe biblical illiteracy. In seeking to delve into the Bible, however, Christians would do well to alter their approach. Instead of plowing through Bible-in-a-year reading plans, students should embrace a long-term approach and focus on delving deeper into individual book studies. One such approach is the Seven-Year Bible Reading Plan.

Study Questions:

1. What is your present relationship to God's Word?

   a. What is your regular reading and study plan?

   b. What are some of the challenges that you have faced in approaching the Bible?

2. What have you observed about our current spiritual climate in America? Why do you think fewer people are reading their Bibles?

3. How did David, Jeremiah, and Ezekiel describe their relationship to God's Word?

4. What are the benefits and drawbacks of Bible-in-a-Year reading plans? What are the potential benefits of taking a longer, slower approach?

5. What are the two ditches we ought to avoid in studying our Bibles?

BEGINNING
WITH PRAYER

Many of us know the old adage: *How do you eat an elephant? Answer: One bite at a time.* But that advice still does not diminish the overwhelming feeling of attempting such a gargantuan feat. In fact, regardless of all the pithy sayings in the world, the mere sight of a 12,000-pound beast on a dinner plate would be enough to send even the hungriest person screaming for the hills. Bible study can often feel the same way.

It is not uncommon for new students of the Bible to feel overwhelmed and even lost regarding how to begin their exploration of Scripture. The sight of a thousand crisp, unread pages has scared off numerous timid believers, and frustrated even the most earnest of them. The problem is not that they aren't desiring to know the Bible—*they're starving!* Rather, the problem is often that they don't know where to begin. Coupled with the trouble of not knowing how to begin is the fact that many people do not understand the nature of the book they're trying to read.

Quite simply, the Bible is a unique book. To most people in the world today, the Bible is merely an ancient book, full of archaic verses and fantastical stories—a collection of old fables and clever maxims. In their naivety, many people hold the view that the Bible generally comprises nothing more than nice thoughts about God. Folks call it "The Good Book"—that is, a book *so good* that most people don't bother to read it! Even many Christians, while they may recognize the Bible to be important, struggle to understand the true *nature* of the Bible and why it is so precious. And so, before we can begin to access the Bible, we will do well to explore its unique nature. As you will see, once we understand what the Bible actually is, we can then begin to understand how to access it, understand it, love it, and be changed by it.

AN INTELLECTUAL BOOK

As a work of literature, the Bible is widely regarded as one of the most amazing documents in all of antiquity. As a complete work, the Bible consists of sixty-six books—thirty-nine in the Old Testament and twenty-seven in the New Testament. However, not all of the books are the same. Some of them are works of history, while others are poetry and wisdom literature. There are biographical accounts, genealogical records, personal letters, and prophetic visions. The Bible was written over the course of nearly sixteen hundred years by more than forty different authors, spanning several geographical regions and speaking multiple languages. When you sit back and think about all that went into the Bible's composition, transmission, and preservation, you cannot help but feel a sense of awe.[1]

In seeking to understand the Bible as a work of literature, a person needs to employ the full use of all their mental faculties. Now, that's not to say that it's *too* difficult—it's certainly no more technical than The Lord of the Rings series, or any other work of enjoyable literature. But it does take a certain amount of mental effort to read and comprehend words, phrases, symbols and imagery, a narrative storyline, and a whole host of complex characters. In fact, great scholars in Ivy League schools have spent whole careers studying the Bible as an invaluable work of timeless literature. However, one cannot approach the study of the Word of God with sheer brain power alone. Why? Because the Bible is more than simply an intellectual book.

A SPIRITUAL BOOK

In addition to being a work of literature, the Bible is also a *spiritual* book—it consists of more than words and punctuation, paper and cowhide. There is a supernatural component to it. While we can trace the historical development of the Bible, it's important to understand that the Bible claims for itself a far more glorious origin.

The Bible itself makes the claim of *divine inspiration*. In his second letter to Timothy, the apostle Paul notes of the power and wisdom of the Bible. He writes, "All Scripture is inspired by God and profitable for teaching, for reproof, for correction, for training in righteousness; so that the man of God may be adequate, equipped for every good work" (2 Tim. 3:16–17). Paul declares the Scriptures to be "inspired by God" (the Greek word *theopneustos* literally means "God-breathed"). It's as though God took a deep breath in, and exhaled Holy Scripture. It's pure revelation proceeding from the mind of God through the mouth of God. Even though we know the books of the Bible were written by more than forty different authors in three different languages spanning several geographical and cultural environments over the course of nearly sixteen hundred years, the Bible claims for itself one divine Author. This is why we call the Bible "God's Word," because when Scripture speaks, God speaks.

How much of the Bible is inspired by God?

The Greek word for "writings" (*graphē*) refers to *all* of "the sacred writings" (v. 15)—that is, the entire Bible. At the time of Paul's letter, the sentiment referred to the Old Testament, but the sentiment is meant to be applied to all of the inspired Scriptures, which includes the New Testament.[2] As Christians, we recognize that the whole Bible, from Genesis to Revelation, is inspired Scripture.

But how did it end up on the page?

Peter helps us understand the process. While some might have tended to believe that the Scriptures were simply religious texts written by religious leaders, the Bible teaches that the Holy Spirit inspires the authors of the Scriptures. We read, "But know this first of all, that no prophecy of Scripture is a matter of one's own interpretation, for no prophecy was ever made by an act of human will, but men moved by the Holy Spirit spoke from God" (2 Peter 1:20–21). Essentially, Peter is saying that Scripture doesn't come to us by human effort or interpretation, but that the Holy Spirit, speaking through the writers' natural voices, superintended the words of Scripture, effectively carrying the writers along in their endeavor. The Bible, therefore, is a spiritual book.

Furthermore, Hebrews 4:12 says that "the word of God is living and active"—the Bible is alive! It's not that the ink and paper is anything special but rather that there is something to the content, *to the words* of Scripture. How can this be? We understand that the same Holy Spirit who inspired the Word of God is also the same Spirit who presently and actively works through the words of Scripture to accomplish His work in the hearts and minds of believers. And so, if the content of the Bible is wholly spiritual, then the readers of the Bible need the help of the Spirit to rightly understand and apply its truths. In other words, we need spiritual eyesight.

SPIRITUAL EYESIGHT

When the apostle Paul wrote his first letter to the church in Corinth, he was keenly aware that he was entering a spiritual and intellectual minefield. Corinth was a cosmopolitan city, marked both by incredible education and learning, as well as grotesque debauchery. First-century Greco-Roman culture valued new ideas and philosophy, and the citizens of Corinth were no different. However, Paul was writing a message to the Corinthian church that would prove not to appeal to the intellectual elite. Early in his letter, he specifically notes that "Jews ask for signs and Greeks search for wisdom; but we preach Christ crucified, to Jews a stumbling block and to Gentiles foolishness" (1 Cor. 1:22–23). Can you believe it?! He calls the message of the gospel *foolishness*!

In declaring the biblical message to be "foolishness," however, Paul adds that God intends to use that "foolish" message "to shame the wise" and "the weak things of the world to shame the things which are strong" (v. 27). In other words, God does not intend to deliver His saving message in such a way that only the smartest people in the world can understand. Otherwise, who could be saved? Only the cultural and intellectual elite. Instead, God provides another means to help us understand His truth—He gives understanding through the ministry of the Holy Spirit. Of this reality, Paul writes,

> *For to us God revealed them through the Spirit; for the Spirit searches all things, even the depths of God. For who among men knows the thoughts of a man except the spirit of the man which is in him? Even so the thoughts of God no one knows except the Spirit of God. Now we have received, not the spirit of the world, but the Spirit who is from*

God, so that we may know the things freely given to us by God, which things we also speak, not in words taught by human wisdom, but in those taught by the Spirit, combining spiritual thoughts with spiritual words.

But a natural man does not accept the things of the Spirit of God, for they are foolishness to him; and he cannot understand them, because they are spiritually appraised. But he who is spiritual appraises all things, yet he himself is appraised by no one. For who has known the mind of the Lord, that he will instruct Him? But we have the mind of Christ. (1 Cor. 2:10–16)

This is what is known as the doctrine of *divine illumination.*

Essentially, *illumination* is when the Spirit of God turns on the lights in your mind. When a person is born again, they receive the Holy Spirit who indwells them; He takes up residence in your heart and mind. As a new creation, you are then able, *by the Spirit*, to see things you've never seen before, and understand what was once unclear and confusing. We see this in John 16:13 when Jesus tells the disciples, "When He, the Spirit of truth, comes, He will guide you into all the truth." Furthermore, He continues, "He will take [what is] Mine and will disclose it to you" (v. 14). This promise made by Jesus was specifically pertaining to the disciples' work of receiving the revelation of the New Testament, but it shows us a timeless truth that is applicable for believers today. When a Christian reads the Bible and understands, it's because the Holy Spirit is giving them spiritual eyesight. Perhaps you know what I'm talking about. Has there ever been a time you've read a verse or a passage over and over again until, one day, it just seems to "open up" and start to make sense? That's illumination.

Now, the Spirit of God is able to grant understanding any time He wants. I've met many believers who make a habit of "Bible-surfing"—when you plop down your Bible, flip it open indiscriminately, and hope that God will speak to you. Now, it's not outside the realm of possibility that God could use a random verse to speak to you, but it's not the most reliable or responsible method for sustainable Christian growth.

So how do I begin? It might seem like the obvious first step would be to sit down and throw open your Bible, but, truthfully, the first thing you ought to do is ask for help. Before you start noodling around, I encourage you to begin with prayer.

BEGINNING WITH PRAYER

You may be thinking, *Why is he taking time to define and discuss prayer? I know how to pray!* That may very well be, but too many believers misunderstand and misappropriate prayer and Bible reading; others skip it completely. In fact, prayer is an essential component to Bible study—perhaps the *most* important part! So let's spend some time delving into prayer and its role in Bible study.

We need to start by getting some basics down. *What is*

prayer? At its core, prayer is our talking to God. But it's more than that. John Piper writes, "Prayer is the open admission that without Christ we can do nothing. And prayer is the turning away from ourselves to God in the confidence that He will provide the help we need."[3] It is, as David models for us, asking God to "search me . . . and know my heart; try me and know my anxious thoughts; and see if there be any hurtful way in me, and lead me in the everlasting way" (Ps. 139:23–24). When we pray, we are talking to God, asking Him, even pleading with Him, for help and guidance. Our hearts want to be closer to Him and to know Him better.

Sometimes the question is posed: *If God knows everything, then why pray?* It's easy to reason this way: *When it comes to Bible study, won't God just help me understand?* Certainly, God wants believers to understand the Bible! But again, prayer is humbly asking God for help. It's an act of faith; it's an act of looking to Him for guidance. Whereas it would be easy for us to wade into self-sufficiency or even arrogance in thinking we could simply figure it out, approaching Bible study with prayer places our trust in the Author of the Scriptures, and asks Him to give us His spiritual eyesight.

HOW DOES PRAYER WORK?

Perhaps the most famous prayer in the Bible is Jesus' prayer in Matthew 6. Known by many as the "Our Father" or "The Lord's Prayer," this model of prayer provides Jesus' instructions to His disciples on how to pray. Now, we understand that His prayer is not a formula to be endlessly recited; otherwise His admonition against meaningless repetition in verse 7 wouldn't make much sense. Rather, Jesus teaches us how to pray by giving us a model. And in His model prayer, one of the petitions is for the Lord to provide food, even spiritual food—"give us this day our daily bread" (v. 11). And so, if it's important to Jesus to ask the Father to feed us, even spiritually, we ought to take it to heart as well.

But what is it that we're actually praying for when we ask God to illumine us? In essence, we're asking that the Father would take His revealed Word and implant it into our souls so that we will grow spiritually. And so, a prayer to God to be fed is a prayer for God to do supernatural work in our heart and soul. Don't take this lightly—this is a radical concept. We're asking God to do something in us that no moral self-improvement regimen can do, what no government institution can do, what no earthly interpersonal relationship can do. We're asking God to remake us from the inside out. Yet too many believers are sheepish with this prayer. Prayer isn't an exercise in wishful thinking. It's an act of faith.

When Abraham was first told that he would become the father to a child in his old age, he was overjoyed. At first, his wife Sarah didn't quite believe it. But the apostle Paul notes that "without becoming weak in faith he contemplated his own body, now as good as dead since he was about a hundred years old, and the deadness of Sarah's womb" (Rom. 4:19). What God was promising seemed impossible, but we read that "he did not waver in unbelief but grew strong in faith, giving glory to God, and being fully assured that what God had promised, He was able also to perform" (vv. 20–21). I love verse 21 because I believe it best summarizes true faith—*being fully assured that God is able to perform what He has promised*. And when we pray, we need to pray with faith, being fully convinced and assured in our minds that God is able to do the things He has promised to do in the Bible.

What has He promised to do? Among other things, He will sanctify us by the truth of the Word (see John 17:17). He promises to grow us in Christlikeness, from the inside out. But despite His promise to work in us, we are still told to "pray without ceasing" (1 Thess. 5:17). And so, as it pertains to our Bible study, what sort of things should we be praying for?

WHAT SHOULD I PRAY FOR?

Too often, I find it difficult to know what to pray for. I suspect I'm not unlike other Christians. I know I need to pray, but the specifics are sometimes a bit fuzzy to me. In studying the Bible, what kinds of things should we pray for? There may be a myriad of things you could pray for, but let me offer just a few ideas.

Pray for Understanding

In the introduction of his letter to the Colossians, the apostle Paul tells the church that he and his companions have been praying specifically for them. What were they praying for? He writes, "We have not ceased to pray for you and to ask that you may be filled with the knowledge of His will in all spiritual wisdom and understanding" (Col. 1:9). Paul knows that the Christians in Colossae desperately need spiritual wisdom and discernment, as they are being raked over the coals by false religion. However, before he launches into two chapters of correction, he appeals to the Lord to grant them both wisdom and understanding.

While there may be much that we may be able to figure out on our own, we must remember that the Bible is a spiritual book. God is the One who can enlighten the eyes of our hearts (see Eph. 1:18) and "[make] wise the simple" (Ps. 19:7). As we saw earlier, through the ministry of the Holy Spirit, God grants spiritual understanding. Even if a verse may seem straightforward, ask the Lord to give you better and deeper understanding. And when a verse or a passage seems impossible to understand, pray that the Lord would help you understand.

Pray for Wisdom

Just like with understanding, we are also told to ask the Lord for wisdom. What is wisdom? One definition that I've come to love is: *wisdom is the right application of knowledge.* It's taking what you have learned and putting it to good and proper use. This is a very important component to studying the Bible. But how important?

Scripture specifically tells us that we should pray for

wisdom. James writes, "But if any of you lacks wisdom, let him ask of God, who gives to all generously and without reproach, and it will be given to him" (James 1:5). We see this demonstrated by King Solomon in 1 Kings 3:2–15, where the Lord told him in a dream, "Ask what you wish Me to give you" (v. 5). Solomon could have asked for anything: health, status, power, money, and more. But instead, he asked the Lord to give him wisdom. The Lord granted his request (and more!), which eventually bore fruit on the pages of Scripture in the book of Proverbs. In fact, Proverbs 3:5 specifically tells us, "Do not lean on your own understanding," and instead to trust the Lord to give us all that we need.

Pray for Desire

A prayer for desire is both an earnest prayer and an honest prayer. It's earnest because it asks the Lord to give you a longing and a desire to hear directly from Him in His Word. It's also an honest prayer because it admits that you don't have the level of desire that you know you need to have. How do you pray for this? It could be something as simple as, *Lord, I don't desire You the way I ought to. But please give me a greater desire for You and for Your Word.* I've prayed this prayer many, many times. But it's not magic. There's no formula. It's not about the words; it's about the heart behind it.

I've been through dry seasons in my spiritual life when I've become so desperate for the Lord that I feel like Jacob in Genesis 32 when he wrestles with the Lord, saying, "I will not let you go unless you bless me" (v. 26). At times, my prayer has been, *I won't stop praying until you give me desire for Your Word!* But God is not stingy or ungracious; He is faithful. I truly believe that this is one prayer that God *will* answer favorably. I believe that if you "pray without ceasing" (1 Thess. 5:17), God will eventually ignite a spark in your heart that will cause it to burn with fresh desire for His Word. How long will it take until you begin to experience it? It's hard to say. But don't stop praying until He grants your desire.

Pray for Enjoyment

People do what they enjoy. I think all too often we tend to treat our Bible study like a laborious, joyless exercise. It almost becomes like penance for us, a self-flogging exercise that pleases God at the expense of our own pain. But may it never be! Psalm 1:2 notes that a person is blessed whose "delight is in the law of the LORD, and in His law he meditates day and night." God's desire is for our joy and delight to be in His revealed Word.

My good friend Mack Tomlinson once told me that the reason most people don't read their Bible is because they don't enjoy it. To combat this problem, he suggests praying to the Lord for help in enjoying your Bible study: *Lord, help me enjoy Your Word!*

In the midst of Job's sadness and despair, his friend Elihu ministers to him in a series of four speeches. Designed to correct Job's faulty theology, he encourages Job to "pray to God, and He will accept him, that he may see His face with joy" (Job 33:26). In many ways, we behold the Lord God as He reveals Himself in Scripture, and we would do well to pray that when we see Him, we would have joy. E. M. Bounds writes, "We find . . . the power of prayer to create a real love for the Scriptures, and to put within men a nature which will take pleasure in the Word."[4]

Pray for Change

When we read and study our Bibles, we don't want it to be merely an intellectual exercise. Certainly, we want to gain understanding and wisdom, but we also need to have the truth and wisdom of Scripture permeate our souls and change us from the inside out. In His High Priestly Prayer, Jesus specifically prayed to the Father for His disciples. Of the many things He asked, He prayed, "Sanctify them in the truth; Your word is truth" (John 17:17). To be *sanctified* means to be changed and conformed to the image of Christ; it's growing in personal holiness. We understand Jesus' prayer to be for God to change the disciples from the inside out using His Word.

We would do well to pray for the same thing Jesus prays for—that we would be sanctified, changed from the inside out. We also pray that God would identify sinful behaviors and offenses, bring them to our minds, grant us repentance, and then begin to transform us by renewing our minds with the Scriptures (see Rom. 12:1–2). This is what David prays for in Psalm 139:

> *Search me, O God, and know my heart;*
> *Try me and known my anxious thoughts;*
> *And see if there be any hurtful way in me,*

And lead me in the everlasting way.
(vv. 23–24)

This is nothing short of David's prayer for God to change him. It's an earnest prayer; it's the right prayer. And it's a prayer that can be answered by way of a deep devotion to the study of God's Word.

Summary: Studying the Bible can feel overwhelming, like eating an elephant. To combat this feeling, students need to better understand the Bible as both an *intellectual* book and a *spiritual* book. To better understand Scripture spiritually, Christians need spiritual understanding given by the Lord Himself. To acquire it, you must prayerfully ask. Pray for understanding, wisdom, desire, enjoyment, and change.

Study Questions:

1. In what ways is the Bible an intellectual book?

2. In what ways is the Bible a spiritual book?

3. How do we receive spiritual understanding?

4. What is prayer?

5. What kinds of virtues related to Bible study should we pray for?

CHAPTER THREE

READ:
WHAT DOES IT SAY?

O ur family often travels to the coast of Maine on our days off. After driving only an hour, we are able to visit a truly beautiful place, a place I've been traveling to since I was a boy. Having traveled to the Maine coast all my life, I don't just bring my family to all the tourist traps. Over time, you discover hidden places and little out-of-the-way gems. One of our favorite places is Perkins Cove in Ogunquit. Only a few short sidestreets off the main road, it's a regular hotspot for us. As you snake down the narrow road, you eventually get to a small parking lot, which sits next to the entrance of an innocuous little sign that reads: Marginal Way.

What most people don't know is that Marginal Way is a one-and-a-quarter mile long footpath that hugs the seacoast. As you traverse the winding path, you stand face-to-face with breathtaking views of the Atlantic Ocean. Dotted with inlets, rock faces, lush trees, and gardens, it's our own little heaven on earth. Toward the end of the walk, you are presented with a view of one of the public beaches, which is always overcrowded with tourists. While there's nothing wrong with the tourist spots, most people never go beyond them and take the opportunity to explore the hidden sights, sounds, and smells of Marginal Way. They've simply never ventured off the well-worn paths to discover the deeper beauties.

Bible reading is much like this. So often we tend to visit only Scripture's "hot spots"; we drive by verses and passages so fast that we never get to explore the hidden beauty of what's there. In this chapter, we will discuss the act of reading the Bible, offering best practices and helpful tips. However, before we dive right in, it's important that we understand a few things about the *truthfulness* of God's Word.

THE TRUTHFULNESS OF SCRIPTURE

Without realizing it, we make judgments about everything we read. Even while processing the content of what's in front of us, we are also evaluating the truthfulness of what we are reading. Depending on the trustworthiness of the source, we will ask varying kinds of questions. If we trust the source, we will ask a lot more *how* and *why* questions. However, if we are skeptical of truthfulness of the source, we will intuitively ask questions of viability: *Is this true?*

The Bible itself claims to be true. This is what scholars call the *veracity* of Scripture. If the Bible was truly inspired by God, and those who penned its content were superintended

by the Holy Spirit, then God is the Author of Scripture. And
if we understand that God is the God of truth (Isa. 65:16;
John 3:33; Rom. 3:4; etc.), then His revealed Word must
also be completely true.

But can it be trusted? Bible scholar Robert Saucy is careful to note that "when full consideration is given to the statements of Scripture in light of their intended meaning and
use by the human authors, the Bible is fully trustworthy in
all it states."[1] Further, Psalm 19:7 says of the Scriptures, "the
law of the LORD is perfect, restoring the soul." Note that the
psalmist doesn't just say "truthful" but "perfect," reflecting
its own inerrancy. Psalm 119:160 affirms, "The sum of Your
word is truth, and every one of Your righteous ordinances is
everlasting." This highlights the totality of God's Word being
truthful, as well as timeless. Jesus prayed that the Father
would "sanctify [believers] in the truth," then clarifying,
"Your word is truth" (John 17:17). Again, a bold declaration
that God's Word *is* truth. Paul told Timothy to work hard at
studying and teaching the Word of God, calling it "the word
of truth" (2 Tim. 2:15; see also Eph. 1:13). Over and over
again, the Scriptures bear witness to their own truthfulness.

If the Bible is truly inspired by God, who is Himself true
(Rom. 3:4) and unable to lie (Heb. 6:18), then it is also
truthful and reliable, unable to err. And so, as we read the
Bible, we can have confidence that what we're reading is true.
More than this, it is the revealed Word of the living God.

PREPARING TO READ

My first venture into ministry was shepherding young men's discipleship groups. For many it was the first time anyone had ever come alongside them to teach them the foundations of the Christian life. I distinctly remember one man confessing to me that he was struggling to grow spiritually despite being in his Bible every day. After a few probing questions, we identified the problem. While he was consistent in his Bible reading, he was trying to do it late at night after a long day of work, while watching the game, sandwiched between innings while the TV commercials were muted. It quickly became obvious to him that he wasn't doing all he could do to properly prepare himself to study the Word of God.

But I believe that a large number of believers would immediately improve their time reading the Bible simply by being more prepared. Therefore, a few tips may help set you up for better success in your study.

Carve Out the Time

One of the most common objections for why people don't do the things they're supposed to do is that they claim that they don't have the time. However, we do the things that are most important to us. We *find* the time. More than this, we *make* the time. If I offered you a million dollars to read your Bible every day for the next year, would you do it? Of course you would! You would make the time. You would move mountains to make sure you didn't skip a day. Now consider that knowing the God of the universe is worth more than all the money in the world. Are we any less motivated to make time for Him?

There will always be things fighting for your time. Be intentional. Pick a time that you plan to sit and read. Keep in mind that it does not need to be hours upon hours, but certainly more than just a minute or two. Perhaps consider starting with thirty minutes. As you build your habit, you can add more time as you go. In doing this, you need to know yourself. Are you a morning person? Are you a night owl? If you find yourself leaning toward carving out time at night, consider that if you wait all day before spending time in God's Word, not only will you have less energy and focus, but you will also have labored through the day without eating your spiritual breakfast!

I encourage you to make time in the morning. Set your alarm a half hour earlier, and start your day with God. As you build this habit, you'll actually start to look forward to the time. Tie your Bible time with your morning cup of coffee (or tea) and let it become a natural rhythm for you. When our children were younger, they were up before the donut maker! And so we had to get creative. My wife and I would alternate mornings, where one of us would get up with the kids and the other would spend time doing Bible study. And then, on the off mornings, we would follow up later to fill in what we missed. At the time, it wasn't ideal, but it was a consistent habit, and we both looked forward to having that time. Our children are a little older now, and we've been able to build in a morning routine where they get themselves up and make their own breakfast while Jess and I have our time in the Bible. Then, after we've had time, we bring them in for a morning devotional. We're not the model family by any stretch, but we've worked hard to set our priorities and carve out time in the mornings for the Lord.

Find a Quiet Place

Once you have decided when you plan to read your Bible, you also need to find a place to sit and learn from the Lord. Don't buy into the delusion that you can have your time with God in front of the TV. If possible, find a quiet nook in your house somewhere. That may be the living room couch, at an office desk, or in the basement. I have a friend who took "prayer closet" literally, emptied out his bedroom closet, and stuck a chair and lamp inside so that he could have his quiet time. Truly, it doesn't matter. Be creative. Be deliberate. And if you have a family, be lovingly explicit about your desire to make this work. Even if you have to sit in your car, find a quiet place.

Remove Distractions

Next, you will need to remove any and all distractions. As technology advances, we seem to find more and more things by which we can be distracted. But as you carve out time and find a quiet place, work hard to remove all distractions.

For many people, that involves not having their phone next to them. A good rule of thumb may be that you commit to spending time in the Word of God before reading emails or posting on social media. What about your family?

I want to be emphatic on this point: if you have children, they ought *not* to be treated as "distractions"—they are God's gracious gift to you to steward and shepherd well. There is also a danger of focusing so much on them that you neglect your personal spiritual responsibilities. Susanna Wesley (mother to John and Charles) had ten children bustling about in her house every day. However, she had trained them to give her time with the Lord every day. How did she do that? She would sit at her kitchen table and pull her apron over her head. When her children saw their mother at the table praying under her apron, they knew not to bother her until she was finished. You may need to be creative with how you manage distractions around you. But I would add that when it comes to children, one of the greatest things you can teach them is that time with God is supremely important. And when they grow up, they will remember having a parent who started the day seeking the Lord.

Pray Before You Read

As we saw in the previous chapter, it is crucial to pray before—and I would add after—you read your Bible. This is an exercise of reliance on the Spirit of God to give understanding to the believer. You don't need to prostrate yourself on the floor for hours before you read your Bible (despite the fact that it may be profitable for us once in a while). Rather, you simply want to bow your head, quiet your mind, and ask the Lord for understanding. You will find that He is always eager to reward those who earnestly seek Him (Heb. 11:6).

PLANNING TO READ

There are two common approaches to Bible reading today. The first approach consists in starting with the book of Genesis and trying to plow through to Revelation. This approach treats the Bible like other long books, as simply a work of literature that must be read sequentially. But we know that the Bible is different. Some portions of the Bible are poetic, others prophetic, and not everything is laid out in chronological order. Certainly, there are benefits to reading the Bible straight through from Genesis to Revelation (as we'll discuss shortly), but I will argue that there may be a better way.

The second approach is simply to throw open the Bible and spot-read a passage or book. Sometimes this is done intentionally: "I feel like reading Proverbs today." Other times it's done out of a sense of feeling overwhelmed or unsure: "I'm not sure what to do, so I'm just going to flip open to a random passage and hope it proves helpful to me today." R. C. Sproul called this approach "luckydipping." He explained, "Luckydipping refers to the method of Bible study in which a person prays for divine guidance and then lets the Bible fall open to whatever it happens to open. Then with eyes shut the person 'dips' a finger to the page and gets an answer from God wherever the finger lands on the page."[2] Again, we know that "all Scripture . . . is profitable" (2 Tim. 3:16) and God's Word never returns void (Isa. 55:11), but these two approaches create gaps in our biblical understanding and often do not help us grow completely. Countless believers for centuries have tended to approach their Bible reading with a much more systematic approach.

Reading the Bible in a Year

For years many Christians have adopted a very simple, straightforward method of reading the whole Bible all the way through in one calendar year. There are several versions of this method,[3] but the general principle is the same: read the whole Bible every year. Writing in 1879, J. C. Ryle noted his preferred method:

> *I believe it is by far the best plan to begin the Old and New Testaments at the same time, to read each straight through to the end, and then begin again. This is a matter in which every one must be persuaded in his own mind. I can only say it has been my own plan for nearly forty years, and I have never seen cause to alter it.*[4]

Of course, it's hard to argue with the testimony of an esteemed English pastor! There is tremendous wisdom and immeasurable blessing in reading the Bible straight through each year. Engaging in this kind of method ensures that you're accessing the Word of God every day and exposing yourself to the whole counsel of God on a regular basis. In fact, if you do nothing else but read through the whole Bible every year for the rest of your life, the Lord will surely use His Word to instruct, convict, sanctify, and bless you! Even if you were to stop reading this book here and committed to reading the Bible yearly, I could die a happy pastor.

That said, I want to suggest another method for reading and studying the Bible.

Seven Year Bible Study Method

Back in chapter 1, I introduced the Seven Year Bible Study method, along with a few lines of argument. You may also want to read the appendix to see how I took this journey myself. But the basic premise of this method of study is to offer a paradigm shift in thinking about learning the Bible. Instead of resetting your reading (and thinking) about the Bible every year, adjust your thinking for a longer term approach. The goal is greater retention and deeper understanding.

As you sit with a single book of the Bible (or portion of a book), your affinity and interest deepens. As you read the words, verses, and passages over and over again consistently, your familiarity of them grows. At the end of one week, you will develop a good working understanding of what's going on in the passages. At the end of two weeks, your critical thinking of the verses begins to intensify. And at the end of one month in the same section of Scripture, it becomes an old friend that you're sad to leave when you move on to the next book of the Bible.

Whereas reading the whole Bible in a year is certainly profitable, committing to a longer view of study has the ability to transform your Christian walk. While it's certainly more ambitious than other plans, something happens when you change your focus. You begin to relax and settle into your study. The journey changes from a year-long marathon across flat ground to a longer, slower trek up a beautiful mountain with magnificent views all along the way. As your commitment level grows daily, you immerse yourself deeper into the well of God's revelation. Do you want to learn joy? Spend a month in Philippians. Do you want to understand the gospel? Spend a month in Galatians; spend three months in Romans! Do you want to stand in awe of the Lord Jesus Christ? A year in the Gospels will leave you breathless.

In the end, there is no wrong way to read the Bible. God has blessed believers' commitment to Scripture for thousands of years. Rather, it's about our hearts. It's about dedication and developing a love for God through reading His Word.

A WORD ABOUT TRANSLATIONS

The Bible was written in two primary languages, Hebrew and Greek, though some small portions were written in Aramaic. Unless you're fluent in those languages, you will likely be reading a translation into your own language. One common question I hear is: *What translation should I use?* It's a good question with many answers. The short answer is: *it depends.* Each English translation has its own purpose and philosophy. I like to think of them as tools on a tool belt; each one has a different function and can be useful to the believer.

Essentially, there are two main translation philosophies. The first is called *formal equivalence,* also known as "essentially literal." In a nutshell, the goal of this approach is to try and translate word for word from the Hebrew or Greek text and create an edition that is as close to the original text without sacrificing readability. There are several English translations that take this approach such as the New American Standard Bible, the New King James Version, the Christian Standard Bible, and the English Standard Version. These versions attempt to be precise and accurate to the original text.

The second philosophy is called *dynamic equivalence,* and seeks to give a more thought-for-thought translation of the Bible. The theory behind this approach is to give a more modern sense to an ancient book. It seeks to render difficult words and phrases into English equivalents that make it easier for the modern reader to understand. The English translations that embrace this philosophy are the New International Version, the Contemporary English Version, and the New Living Translation.

Admittedly, these Bible translations exist on a spectrum, and some (like the NIV) are closer to the literal side than others. While I appreciate the helpful clarity of some of the dynamic equivalence translations, I prefer and recommend students of Scripture to use a more essentially literal translation. My reason for this is that I believe Christians should be reading versions that are as close to God's revealed Word as humanly possible. I want to understand the mind of God. I want to be able to study the Scripture in the spirit of how it was written. Further, whatever clarity is gained by modernizing words and phrases can be easily picked up by utilizing a Bible dictionary or commentary. As a believer, I want to read God's Word with as little obstruction as possible; I want to eat unprocessed spiritual food.[5]

READING

A cursory Google search will reveal a plethora of articles about how to read. People often struggle with practicing the right method of reading in order to better understand the text in front of them. What is the best approach? Slow or fast? Scanning or searching? While you may desire to explore the theories behind the practice of reading,[6] for the purpose of Bible study, I encourage you to vary your approach. Perhaps start by reading the text at a comfortable pace in order to get the context and the flow of what's written. Then when you have a general sense of the content, go back and read more slowly to begin to examine it more deeply.

Because at the heart of Bible reading is the question: *What does it say?* Remember, the goal is not simply to get through it or to walk away with merely a general sense of the verses. The goal is understanding. Therefore, read with a view to understanding. In order to understand the text, we need to read the Bible carefully, even assiduously.

The word *assiduous* means to do something with great care, attention, and persistence. While use of the word has declined the past few hundred years, it describes a timeless virtue that is needed for Bible study. To read the Scriptures *assiduously* means that you approach the texts with great care, intense scrutiny, and unrelenting vigor. It's where you grab a verse and wrestle with it until you understand why it's there. Eighteenth-century New England pastor Jonathan Edwards offered this encouragement: "Be assiduous in reading the holy Scriptures. This is the fountain whence all knowledge in divinity must be derived. Therefore let not this treasure lie by you neglected."[7]

At the heart of careful (and *assiduous*) reading is the active work of examination and making observations of what is in the text.

Observation

It's important to read with your eyes open. What do I mean by that? When we feel foggy or distracted, our minds tend to wander, and we're not really paying attention. But if we are able to focus on what we're reading and be present with the text, we have a much better chance to understand and retain it.

As you read, you want to make observations. You want to make note of what you see in the text itself. While not attempting to be exhaustive in your observations,[8] begin by taking note of the following:

Proper Names and Places. It's important to identify the writer of the historical text, as well as the subject. Who wrote the book? Who are the people involved in the story or letter? In addition, identify the geographic location and immediate location in order to understand the proper setting.

Key Words. Often, this may be a theological word that sits at the heart of a verse or passage. For example, *justified* in Galatians 2:16, or *propitiation* in 1 John 2:2. When you move to interpret the passage, these key words will be invaluable to know. Identifying and understanding key terms will help you grasp the big idea of the passage.

Repeated Words. Many times in the Bible, key words are repeated for emphasis ("Holy, holy, holy" in Isa. 6:3, for example) or repeated because they are expounded as a key theme in a passage ("comfort" in 2 Cor. 1:3–7, for instance). When you see repeated terms, think about what such repetition points to.

Grammar. It's very important when making observations of the Bible that you make note of verbs (action words), figures of speech, and conjunctions. Consider also how people and concepts are connected. And pay special attention to terms such as "so that" and "therefore."

In the end, your goal is to open your eyes and see everything you possibly can in the text. Ask clarifying questions of the text. *Who is speaking? Where does this take place? Why did this happen?* Try to figure out what's going on. Get the story or argument of the passage in your mind so that you can think more deeply about it. And as you think, you can meditate on it.

Meditation

As you read, you want to work hard to get the Bible into your mind. There's nothing worse than spending thirty minutes reading your Bible only to forget everything you read on your drive to work. You want it to stick. One key way of doing that is to *meditate* on what you read.

At the most basic level, meditation is the act of mental chewing. It's the practice of turning words and phrases over in your mind. Admittedly, the act of biblical meditation will naturally lead you to interpretation (which we will cover in the next chapter), but this is no less an important part of understanding what you're reading.

In order to help illustrate biblical meditation, let's look at an example. In Matthew 16:18, the Lord Jesus makes a power-packed statement about the church. This is one of those verses that has been read, studied, memorized, and debated for centuries. While talking with His disciples, after Peter's confession of faith, Jesus remarks, "I will build My church; and the gates of Hades will not overpower it." Let's take a look at the phrase "I will build My church." In turning it over in your mind, one technique that proves helpful in seeing this phrase from many different angles is the practice of emphasizing different words in the verse. As you alternate your emphasis, it looks like this:

I will build My church.
I *will* build My church.
I will *build* My church.
I will build *My* church.
I will build My *church*.

As you carefully repeat and emphasize each word, take what you've observed already in reading the passage in order to understand this one phrase. First, we note that the "*I*" refers to Jesus Himself. Next, we see that the word "*will*" indicates His infrustratible determination to accomplish the task. Next, we see that He will "*build*" His church; this is positive construction. Then He asserts His ownership, calling it "*My* church." Lastly, we are introduced for the first time to the word "*church*" in Matthew's gospel, which we will soon discover to be the collective assembly of Christian believers. In our example, we have not yet determined what the phrase *means*—that's the process of *interpretation*. But by meditation, we are able to observe what's going on in the text, as well as raise for ourselves some good questions that need to be answered as we move ahead.

On the practice of Bible meditation, J. C. Ryle writes,

> *Let us resolve to* meditate more on the Bible. *It is good to take two or three texts with us when we go out into the world, and to turn them over and over in our minds whenever we have a little leisure. It keeps out many vain thoughts. It tightens the nail of daily reading. It preserves our souls from stagnating and*

*breeding corrupt things. It sanctifies and
quickens our memories, and prevents
them becoming like those ponds where
the frogs live but the fish die.*[9]

It's difficult to overstate the benefits of meditating on Scripture, but as we've seen, it's essential for the purpose of understanding, as well as for transforming our minds in the way of godliness.

Memorization

In my view, the last real exercise pertaining to reading is *memorization*. In doing this, you're now working to get the Bible into your heart. Of all the verses in the Bible that call for memorization, Psalm 119:11 is surely the most famous. It reads, "Your word I have treasured in my heart, that I may not sin against You." Some translations render "treasured" as "hidden" or "stored up"—the idea being that the believer has locked the Scripture away deep inside their heart in order to keep it forever. Elsewhere, God told Joshua, "This book of the law shall not depart from your mouth, but you shall meditate on it day and night, so that you may be careful to do according to all that is written in it" (Josh. 1:8). The point is clear: If we are to live as Christians, we are to make regular practice of hiding God's Word in our hearts.

But how do we do this?

The discipline of memorization is the act of committing Scripture to memory in order to be recalled at a later time.

As for the best method, there are countless practices that aid in memorization.

Flashcards. This is a tried and true method of learning information. Simply buy a stack of 3x5-inch index cards and write verses out in full, along with the verse address. These are easy to carry in your pocket, or to post up on your bathroom mirror or computer screen at work. The idea is that you can take a few verses with you wherever you go and practice reciting them until you have them locked in your mind.

The Topical Memory System. The Topical Memory System was developed by The Navigators and has been used by countless Christians for decades. Essentially, the system organizes key verses into topics in order to cover key doctrines of Christianity. While the system is not designed to be exhaustive, it serves as a sure-fire way to nail down key verses such as Matthew 28:19–20; John 3:16; Romans 1:16; 3:23; 5:8; 6:23; 10:9–10; Galatians 2:20; Ephesians 2:8–9; and more.

Memorization Apps. Modern technology has produced amazing tools for Bible memorization. These days, there's an app for everything. While you can certainly learn the Bible by simply reading it on your phone or mobile device, several apps have been created for that purpose. One app that is particularly helpful for memorization is called *Bible Memory Pro*. It not only helps you learn the verses, but also tracks your progress and includes sharing options so you can give and receive encouragement from friends as you grow.

Be Creative. In the end, you have to know yourself. What works best for you? Not everyone is the same, and there's no wrong way to memorize the Bible. So be creative. Play games with yourself. Make it fun. One summer I wanted to memorize the whole book of Romans. I knew it was a tall order, so I pulled out all the stops. I wrote out notecards with individual verses on them, banded together by chapter. I kept one chapter on me at all times, flipping through the cards over and over again until I felt like I could recite them from memory. In addition, I recorded myself reading the verses so that I could play it back in the car on the way to work each day. This way, I could hear the verses in my own voice and recite along with the recording. It still amazes me how much I was able to squeeze into my brain that summer!

In the end, there are a multitude of ways to get the Bible into your heart and mind. But work hard to read to understand. Don't give up on a verse or a passage until you have a sense of it, even if you don't fully understand what it means. And as you work to develop the discipline of reading, it won't be long before you become anxious to roll up your sleeves and study the Bible even more.

Summary: Because God Himself is true, His Word is also true. Therefore, we understand that the Bible is *inerrant* and *infallible* in all it claims. In seeking to read the Bible faithfully and effectively, we should take great care to prepare our mind, heart, and environment. Reading can be done at many different levels, but it's important to practice making careful observation. In addition, meditating on verses and memorizing portions of Scripture is helpful for internalizing Scripture. In the end, the goal is to hide God's Word in your heart.

Study Questions:

1. How does knowing about the truthfulness of Scripture help you trust more in it?

2. What are some of the suggested preparations that may be made prior to reading?

3. What kinds of observations should be made in reading?

4. Why is systematic reading helpful? What is "luckydipping"?

5. Challege yourself to memorize a verse or a short passage of Scripture.

CHAPTER FOUR

STUDY: WHAT DOES IT MEAN?

A few years ago I had the pleasure of visiting the Museum of Biblical Art in Dallas, Texas. Filled with timeless pieces from history, the museum is a tremendous feast for the eyes and heart. One of the more prominent pieces featured is a giant mural titled *The Resurrection* by painter Ron DiCianni. Standing twelve feet high and forty feet wide, the stunning piece portrays Jesus Christ emerging victoriously from the tomb, surrounded by numerous witnesses from biblical history. Vibrant with color and symbolism, the painting leaves you standing in awe as you behold the glorious depiction of Christ's resurrection.

While touring the museum, we carved out extra time to stop and gaze at *The Resurrection*. Our guide gave us time to look at the painting on our own before he pointed out key features. Beyond the obvious persons portrayed, he noted several other subtle details that we hadn't noticed. The longer we stayed there looking, the more the mural came alive to us. In truth, we could have spent all day there. At face value, you could make a general observation: "It's Jesus coming out of the tomb," and you would be right. But the true meaning of the depicted event is much deeper. There's more going on. It would almost be a crime to walk by such a painting and give it only a quick glance. Likewise, I fear that far too many Christians who read the Scriptures give them only a quick glance. Too often, they don't take the time to stop and gaze at the Scriptures, and examine the true meaning of God's revelation.

The Word of God is meant to be more than tasted; it's meant to be chewed and digested in order that it may nourish us. But with so much history, culture, theology, prophecy, and symbolism embedded in the Scriptures, many people ask, "Can the Bible be understood?" The faithful student must do the work. They must study. In this chapter, we'll explore various tools that can be used to understand the Bible, but before we do that, let's first talk about the clarity of Scripture.

THE CLARITY OF SCRIPTURE

One of the most debated topics during the Protestant Reformation focused on the doctrine of Scripture. One aspect of the argument pertained to the clarity of Scripture. Was the Bible too difficult to be understood by "common" people? The Roman Catholic Church said yes, but Reformers like Martin Luther said no. In his classic work *Bondage of the Will*, Luther attacks the suggestion that the Bible is too difficult to understand. He writes,

> Satan has used unsubstantial spectres
> to scare men off reading the sacred
> text, and to destroy all sense of its value,
> so as to ensure that his own brand of
> poisonous philosophy reigns supreme in
> the church.[1]

Luther rails against not just the notion that the Bible is too difficult to understand, but also sinister reasons why the Bible was being kept from people. Furthermore, he argues for the true source of understanding:

> The profoundest mysteries of the
> supreme Majesty are no more hidden
> away, but are now brought out of doors
> and displayed to public view. Christ
> has opened our understanding, that
> we might understand the Scriptures,
> and the Gospel is preached to every
> creature.[2]

What the Reformers believed, as well as Protestant teachers in subsequent generations, was the clarity of Scripture, also called the *perspicuity* of Scripture.

The Bible itself declares itself to be understandable to believers. While in many ways, the depths of God's wisdom are unsearchable (Rom. 11:33), the Bible states clearly that "the testimony of the LORD is sure, *making wise the simple*"

(Ps. 19:7, emphasis added). Furthermore, Psalm 119:130 affirms that studying the Word of God "gives understanding to the simple." Who are "the simple"? It is a person who "lacks intellectual ability," as well as "one who lacks sound judgment, who is prone to making mistakes, and who is easily led astray."[3] In other words, the Bible is not written merely for the intellectual elite, for scholars and geniuses; it's written for all people, even those of the most limited understanding. Even young children are commanded to be taught the Word of God (Deut. 6:6–7; Eph. 6:4), implying that a certain level of understanding is expected for even the simplest minds.

Despite the Bible's inherent clarity, we also know that the Holy Spirit must give illumination and understanding (see chapter 2). There are deep, hidden truths that are not immediately grasped at the first reading of the Bible. Therefore, the Spirit must give understanding and discernment. However, this is not a mechanical or formulaic process. How much of our understanding of the Bible is based on personal study verses the Spirit's illumination? We have no way of knowing. However, we certainly know that we need both. We are to study hard like the Bereans in Acts 17:11; we must also entrust our minds to the ministry of the Holy Spirit.

We have already discussed the discipline of praying for illumination and understanding. However, in this chapter, we will explore the discipline of studying and interpreting the Word of God.

EXEGESIS AND HERMENEUTICS

In order to faithfully approach the study of Scripture, we must employ the use of two related disciplines. The first is called *exegesis*. Exegesis is "the careful, systematic study of the Scriptures to discover the original, intended meaning."[4] R. C. Sproul notes that "the word comes from the Greek word meaning, 'to guide out of.' The key to exegesis is found in the prefix *ex*, which means 'from' or 'out of.' To exegete Scripture is to get out of the words the meaning that is there, no more and no less."[5] At the heart of exegesis, the Christian disciple seeks to understand what God has intended by what God has written. Therefore, our task is to understand the text of Scripture. This leads to the second discipline: *hermeneutics*.

What is hermeneutics? Gordon Fee and Douglas Stuart write, "Although the word 'hermeneutics' ordinarily covers the whole field of interpretation, including exegesis, it is also used in the narrower sense of seeking the contemporary relevance of ancient texts."[6] Essentially, it is the work of the modern reader to understand ancient writing. To put it even more simply: *hermeneutics is the art and science of interpreting the Bible.* In one way, studying the Bible is an art form that can be developed and honed over years of practice. In another way, it is also a science that operates according to certain rules and disciplines. In the next section, we'll look at some general principles of interpretation, but before we do, we would do well to consider a few truths.

Context Is Key

The first thing we need to consider—and really the overarching principle to all of Bible study—is that *context is key*. This is something seminary professors drill into their students' heads the first year. Bible scholar Robert L. Thomas used to say, "A text without a context is a pretext for a subtext." In other words, if you do not consider the context of what is written, you run the risk of reading something into a text that was never meant to be there.

What is *context*? Context has to do with observing the parts that surround a word or passage in order to shed light on its meaning. To illustrate, my kids are notorious for hearing only pieces of conversations between my wife and me. It's not uncommon for one of my children to run into the room and exclaim, "WE'RE GOING TO DISNEY?!" To which we have to clarify that we're *not*, in fact, going to Disney; they heard only part of the conversation. They didn't hear the words "we" and "Disney" in context.

As it pertains to Bible study, what are some exegetical problems to be aware of?

Errors to Avoid

Eisegesis. Whereas *exegesis* is the extracting of true meaning out of the text, *eisegesis* is the improper reading of one's own subjective meaning back into the biblical text. In other words, it's trying to make a Bible verse or passage mean something that it does not mean. It's helpful to note that "our goal is to grasp the meaning of the text God has intended. We do not create meaning out of a text; rather, we seek to find the meaning that is already there."[7] Eisegesis creates meaning that was never put into the text by God.

Spiritualization. Growing like a weed out of eisegesis is the error of spiritualizing the Bible. At its core, spiritualizing a text is looking for deeper meaning than what might actually be there. I remember hearing the story of a speaker at a Christian youth camp who was teaching on dating, courtship, and marriage. At the end of his message, he instructed each young man in the room to find a girl he wanted to marry, physically march around her seven times, and then, like the walls of Jericho (Josh. 6:15–20), the walls of her heart would come crashing down and she would agree to marry him. As funny as this story may seem, it reveals the foolishness of over-spiritualizing a biblical text. In truth, I think this error is often done with noble intentions—desiring to draw as much spiritual nourishment from a Bible verse as possible. However, this actually damages the true meaning, and robs the reader from God's intended spiritual value. In the end, we simply do not have the authority or license to create new, spiritualized meanings from the Bible.

Over-Personalization. The natural and logical end of eisegesis and spiritualization is the error of *over-personalization*. In short, it's the practice of reading your own personal situation directly into the text. As we'll see in the next chapter, this is different from *application*. We are certainly meant to apply God's Word to our lives, but we are never permitted to make ourselves the focus of the Bible.

I was once told about a woman who was racked with fear and concern over her troubled son. While in Bible study one morning, she read Psalm 37:37: "Mark the blameless man, and behold the upright; for the man of peace will have a posterity." Since her son's first name was Mark, the woman immediately believed that God was speaking directly to her through the verse to reassure her that, despite his drug problem, he would be okay in the end. However, Psalm 37:37 is not about a troubled young man named Mark; it's about God's promise to reward the righteous despite the prevalence of wicked people in the world. And while it's good to seek comfort from the Lord in the midst of difficult circumstances, it's important to treat Scripture faithfully and not read something into the text that is not there.

To avoid problems of eisegesis in our study, we need to make sure we keep everything in its proper context. Once we have this in mind, we can proceed to the principles of interpretation.

PRINCIPLES OF INTERPRETATION

I'll be honest with you. I've read books on Bible study that were so loaded with terms and buzzwords, steps and processes that I walked away feeling totally overwhelmed and inadequate to the task. Certainly, like any serious discipline, Bible study involves a lot. But let me put it into perspective. If you want to learn to love cars, you're going to have to learn a slew of terms and names, as well as an entire skillset for taking apart and putting together a complex machine.

If you want to learn beekeeping, you'll have to learn about bee anatomy and how to maintain hives, as well as the entire science behind the discipline. No matter how you slice it, learning to love something of value is hard work. However, anything worth having is worth working for. So it is with understanding the Word of God.

As for interpreting the Bible, there are numerous concepts to grasp. If we are to love the Bible, we first need to understand it. Even a cursory glance at the best books on understanding God's Word will leave you with columns of terms and principles. While I would certainly encourage you to devote yourself to learning as much as you can about biblical interpretation, here are just a few basic principles to get you off and running.

The Literal Principle

The first and foremost principle of interpreting the Bible is that we are to read it *literally*. This means that you are reading and interpreting Scripture in its normal, natural sense rather than as a mysterious document with various levels of secret meanings behind each text. In interpreting the Bible *literally*, you are seeking to understand the Bible as the kind of literature it is. If you are reading a narrative passage, then understand the text as narrative. If you are reading prophecy, seek to understand those prophetic elements. If you are reading poetic texts, seek to understand it as such. Once you understand the type of literature you are reading, you can interpret the text in its natural sense.

However, there is still a great amount of confusion about this. What about the use of literary devices? A literal reading still takes into account symbols, images, and metaphors. For example, when John the Baptist first realizes who Jesus truly is, he declares, "Behold, the Lamb of God who takes away the sin of the world!" (John 1:29). Now, we know that John was not speaking literalistically—he didn't believe that Jesus was an *actual* lamb! But he was speaking literally, in that the Scriptures attested to the glorious truth that the coming Messiah would function as a sacrifice for His people—a fulfillment of true sacrifice for sins that was only foreshadowed by the Old Testament animal sacrifices. Therefore, in seeing Jesus as the Lamb of God, we understand that He is *literally* the perfect sacrifice for sins.

The Grammatical Principle

The next principle coincides with the first principle, as it considers the *grammatical* components of Scripture. What is grammar? In its most basic sense, grammar is the set of rules that govern language. More specifically, to study grammar is to learn how words and phrases are properly used in a given text. In short, human language has rules, and we are meant to learn them in order to follow them and understand the true meaning of the ideas being expressed.

This is no different with Bible study. We are meant to look at words, phrases, sentences, and paragraphs grammatically. What are the parts of speech? Identify the nouns, verbs, adjectives, adverbs, prepositions, and so on. When you identify the parts of the sentence, you can start to understand what it means. When I started to delve into deeper Bible study, I quickly realized that I didn't understand grammar very well. So I went out and purchased a book on basic grammar, just so that I could understand language a little better.

One of the most challenging and important grammatical distinctions in Scripture is between *indicatives* and *imperatives*. An *indicative* expresses a statement of fact, while an *imperative* expresses a command. The Bible is full of both. One example of this distinction comes to us in Matthew 28:19–20. This is the passage in which Jesus gives the Great Commission: "Go therefore and make disciples of all the nations. . . ." I have often heard well-meaning sermons focus on the word "Go!" as the command. However, the main verb (*mathēteusate*) is "make disciples." This is the *imperative* command. The verbs "go," "baptize," and "teach," are participles of the main verb. And while not the main command, the participles indicate how the command is to be followed. Yet D. A. Carson warns against seeing "go" as having no force behind it[8] (after all, we can't make disciples if we don't go). But the consequence of misunderstanding the Great Commission is that we will think that we're being obedient to the Lord simply by *going somewhere* rather than by *making disciples* wherever we go.

The Historical Principle

When reading the Bible, one thing becomes clear to us: we are reading an ancient book. We are reading about people and events that took place thousands of years ago. However, the largest span between the things we understand today and what took place back then is not an issue of time, but an issue of history and culture. If we are to understand the context of what is written in the Bible, we have to understand the words, phrases, and ideas as they would have been understood by their original hearers.

This is really important because cultures change. How we understand things in modern times is often very different from how things were understood the times of Jesus and the apostles. If we are to read the Bible *historically*, we need to spend a little time learning about what was going on in Bible times. Who is the human writer? To whom was he writing? What were the events taking place at the time? What is the background to the practices being discussed?

Every year our church has a Christmas Eve service. Normally, I take the opportunity to teach through something from the Gospels. One of the key components to the story of the birth of Jesus Christ is the concept of the virgin birth. When we read Matthew's account of the birth of Christ, we are faced with an interpretive challenge. When Joseph discovers that Mary is pregnant, he decides that he is going to "send her away secretly" (Matt. 1:19)—he's going to divorce her. However, when you read the previous verse, we see that they were not yet married but only betrothed to one another. How then could he divorce her? If we are reading our twenty-first century Western concept of marriage into the text, then Joseph and Mary don't appear to be married at all.

But if we do a little historical research into Jewish marriage customs in the first century, we quickly learn that marriage occurred in three stages: the betrothal, the engagement, and the actual marriage ceremony.[9] And while the couple did not consummate their marriage until after the official ceremony, they were already legally married by contract.[10] Therefore, if Joseph believed that Mary had been unfaithful to him, it would constitute a violation of their marriage covenant, and he would have grounds for divorce (see Deut. 24:1–4). Of course, we know that Mary had *not* been unfaithful to her marriage vows; the Child was conceived by the Holy Spirit while she was a virgin. But understanding marriage traditions at the time helps us understand why Joseph believed and acted the way he did.

The Synthesis Principle

The last principle that we will discuss here is called *synthesis*. In general, the word *synthesis* has to do with ideas and concepts working together. When it comes to studying the Bible, we're talking about verses working together—Scripture interpreting Scripture. John Calvin suggests what is called the *analogia scripturae*—the analogy of Scripture (the interpretation of difficult and unclear passages of Scripture with clear passages of Scripture on the same issue).[11] Not only do all the verses work together, no part of the Bible contradicts any other part of it either. Because in the end, God is the best interpreter of His own Word. Therefore, if there are verses that help explain other verses, we would do well to learn from those. Concordances are useful tools to help identify complementary passages that can be understood together. After all, if we understand and believe that God is the supreme Author of Scripture, then it bears true that He would not contradict Himself.

But what about verses that seem to contradict other verses? Certainly there are difficult verses and hard passages. If we understand that God cannot contradict Himself, then we realize that the apparent inconsistency is based on *our* misunderstanding rather than *His* mistake. How, then, do we reconcile difficult verses? It's best to start with what seems most clear and work toward what is more obscure. When we do this carefully and faithfully, we often find that the supposed problem passages are far less problematic than we first thought.

What if we need extra help? That's where outside tools are helpful.

Summary: God has chosen to reveal His truth to us in a way that is clear. And while students can understand the basics of the Bible, the regenerate Christian is enabled by the Holy Spirit to better understand His Word spiritually. The student is able to employ the use of *hermeneutics* to rightly interpret the Bible through *exegesis*—mining the meaning *out of* the Scripture. In studying the Bible using various interpretive principles, the student should seek to understand the context. God has given us various helps in the form of pastors and teachers who provide tools for interpreting and understanding the Bible.

Study Questions:

1. What is the *perspicuity* of Scripture?

2. Explain the connection between exegesis and hermeneutics.

3. What is context, and why is it important?

4. What are the main principles of interpretation?

5. What are some helpful tools to be used in interpretation?

HELPFUL TOOLS

According to Ephesians 4:11, God has given gifts to the church in the form of pastors and teachers. God has been giving understanding and wisdom to countless teachers for thousands of years for the benefit of helping believers in every age know how to live out the Christian life. One reason we have for rejoicing is that, contrary to other disciplines that are constantly needing to update their teaching and textbooks every few years, God's Word never needs updating. Therefore, we can glean helpful insights from Bible teachers in all eras, and be blessed by the innumerable years of their own personal study. Through the years, these teachers have produced many helpful resources and tools to help learners better understand the Bible.

Bible Dictionaries, Encyclopedias, Concordances, Lexicons

There are several books and resources that are essential for Bible study. First, a *Bible dictionary* is a reference work containing entries that explain the people, places, customs, and doctrines of the Bible. Similarly, a *Bible encyclopedia* offers more in-depth entries, often times with fuller articles than the abbreviated entries of dictionaries. Next, a *concordance* is a tool that helps identify verse cross references. While you can purchase these by themselves, most Study Bibles include helpful concordances alongside the text or in the back of the Bible. Lastly, a *lexicon* is a reference tool that helps define Bible words and explain their usage in their original context. These are invaluable for use in word studies.

Study Guides

In addition to Bible tools that help break down and explain individual words, verses, and concepts, there are also a number of very good study guides that have been written to aid in putting it all together. Study guides are more inclusive, helping the student navigate through a whole book of the Bible, and addressing key passages along the way. Study guides often cut out a lot of the preliminary interpretive steps, but still give you an opportunity to study the text for yourself. Sometimes these guides give enough of a boost to keep you moving through the Bible.

Commentaries

A step up from study guides are Bible commentaries. The goal of a commentary is to give helpful systematic explanation and teaching of Bible books. Much like with translations, commentaries are like tools in a tool belt. They each serve their own unique purpose, and they can range from very general to technical. It's wise to consult a commentary after you have done your interpretive work first so as not to become reliant on others' study alone. You want to have the blessing and joy of learning how to study the Bible for yourself. But commentaries can give insights, pose questions, address issues of critical concern, and expose you to academic discussions over debated verses and passages. For my money, commentaries are invaluable when used correctly.

Bible Teachers

While books are often valuable editions to a student's collection, there is often no substitute for a flesh-and-blood teacher. In our modern age, you can really find Bible teaching anywhere on TV or the internet. It's important, however, that you sit under faithful, orthodox teaching. Of course, the most valuable resource you will ever have is your own pastor, who spends week after week ministering the Word of God to the local church. With that said, if you do not have a church that is committed to the faithful weekly exposition of Scripture, I would encourage you to make sure you find a church that does. Far and away, this will help you grow exponentially as a student of God's Word.

As I ponder the blessing of good teachers, my mind often goes to the story of Philip and the Ethiopian eunuch. In Acts 8:30–40, Philip the evangelist meets up with the Ethiopian official who is riding on the back of his chariot with a scroll from Isaiah in his lap. Philip asks the man, "Do you understand what you are reading?" The man responds, "Well, how could I, unless someone guides me?" Without skipping a beat, Philip hopped up next to the man and began explaining not only the meaning of Isaiah 53:7–8 but also how the text pointed to Jesus Christ. This is the real blessing of Bible teachers. As Ephesians 4 says, they are truly gifts to the church.

USEFUL STUDY METHODS

In seeking to grow in their ability to read and interpret the Bible, many believers have found it useful to employ various systematic study methods to help them along. As with nearly everything we've covered in this chapter, these methods are merely tools to aid the student in discovering God's intended meaning in Scripture. In this book, I've advocated for the Seven Year Bible Reading Plan as a foundational method of working through the Word of God, but I recognize that it's only the beginning. There are many methods

of approaching the interpretation of Scripture.[12] The following are two studies that have helped countless believers
through the years as they work to interpret the Scriptures.

Inductive Bible Study

The first study method has been popular for the last few
decades. The inductive Bible study was first made visible
in 1952 by Robert A. Traina in his book, *Methodical Bible
Study*.[13] Since that time, a wide range of books have been
published and popularized by evangelical scholars and
teachers. Following a specific methodological approach,
inductive Bible study focuses on three basic steps: observation, interpretation, and application. While some books
teach the basic principles,[14] other books focus on a specific
method of notetaking and outlining.[15] But this approach to
study has proven itself to be extremely valuable to students
who devote themselves to it.

Topical Bible Study

There is value in a systematic, methodological study of
Scripture—approaches that help the student work through
each book of the Bible in order to develop a full-bodied
understanding of the whole counsel of the Word of God.
But what if you're looking to understand a specific theme
or topic expressed in the Bible? This is where topical Bible
study comes into play. At its core, the Topical approach
traces an individual theme throughout the entirety of Scripture in order to understand the Bible's teaching more completely. For example, if you were interested in learning about
what the Bible teaches about marriage, you would start by
using a concordance or topical study tool and looking up
every applicable reference. This may yield a large number
of references, but try to evaluate their usefulness. In the
marriage example, focus your attention more on Scripture's

teaching on marriage versus only passing references to marriage (for example, "Jacob married Rachel"). Once you have a healthy list of Scriptures, begin using your exegetical tools to understand the Bible's teaching. This systematic, synthetic approach helps you to answer the question: *What does the whole Bible have to say about a topic?* And while you don't want topical studies to constitute the bulk of how you approach the Bible, it is invaluable when you are seeking understanding in a specific area of study.

In the end, the goal is to understand the Bible and un-cover: *What does it mean?* When you become comfortable with helpful study tools, the Bible begins to open up in ways previously unseen through casual reading. However, once we know what the Bible says and means, we next have to understand how to use what we are learning.

CHAPTER FIVE

USE:
HOW DO I APPLY IT?

I remember hearing the story of an old man who lived in a one-room apartment by himself. He never married, and as far as his family could tell, he lived his entire life as a pauper. One day they received word that he had passed away, and so they went to his home to gather what few things he had. When they arrived in his apartment, it was sparse and sad—only a few old rickety pieces of furniture. The walls were relatively bare. Small piles of clutter dotted the room. But when they opened up his closet door, they were met with an astonishing sight. Piled high in the man's closet were bags full of money. By the looks of it, the man had saved virtually every penny he ever earned—hundreds of thousands of dollars. By all rights, he was a rich man who never put his fortune to use for himself, and therefore lived his whole life poor.

Many Christians today, I fear, are much like this poor old man. They have all the treasures of heaven at their fingertips, yet they keep it locked away and never use it. Instead, they live their whole lives as spiritual paupers. What is the remedy for this? It is to take the Word of God and put it to proper use. We must learn to *apply* the Word of God to our lives and therefore realize its benefits. In this chapter, we're going to learn how to apply Scripture. However, we are not meant to use the Word of God selectively or sparingly. The Bible is not merely a book of good advice. As we'll see, the full authority of God is bound up in its pages.

THE AUTHORITY OF SCRIPTURE

One time, I was in a grocery store, and I saw a young boy sitting in his mother's shopping cart. As he was passing through the checkout lane, he grabbed a candy bar out of the rack. Seeing his sly move, his mother told him, "Put that back!" to which he replied, "No! You can't tell me what to do!" To my surprise, the mother caved and let the boy buy the candy bar. Apparently, her authority as a parent didn't stretch very far. This brings up an interesting question for us to consider: *Who has the right to tell us what to do?*

According to Scripture, God Himself possesses full authority over all things, primarily because He created all things. From the opening pages of Genesis 1, God is seen speaking things into existence and then commanding them to conform to His specified plan. The culmination of His creation is that of human beings. In fact, Romans 9 likens our relationship to God as that of a potter and his clay. Does the clay have any right to dictate terms to the potter? Does the clay get a say in how it is made, or what is to be its function? Absolutely not.

Not only do we understand that God created everything that exists; the Bible also states that God owns it all. We read, "The earth is the LORD's, and all it contains, the world, and those who dwell in it" (Ps. 24:1). If God rightly maintains authority over all things, then He has the right to govern those things, to tell those things what to do. How does He communicate His expressed will to His creatures? He does so through His *special revelation*, which Wayne Grudem defines as: "God's words addressed to specific people, including the words of the Bible. This is to be distinguished from general revelation, which is given to all people generally."[1] In other words, general revelation includes what is visible to all people, such as the creation and the human conscience, while special revelation refers to the expressed words of God contained ultimately in Scripture.

Over and over again in the Bible, we read various phrases like, "Thus says the Lord." Often, such phrases are used by an authoritative messenger who is sent to God's people to deliver the Lord's message. Before launching into the details of the message, he would declare, "Thus says the Lord," an indication that what he was about to say came directly from the Lord. And the people knew that, as they listened to the words of the prophet, they were to respond to it as if they were hearing directly from the Lord Himself.

Because the Bible is the inspired, self-revelation of God

written down, every letter bears the full weight of God's authority. Every time you turn to a passage, you are meant to hear "Thus says the Lord" as you're reading. Very simply, when Scripture speaks, God speaks. Therefore, when God speaks to you through His Word, there is the expectation that you will respond to His authoritative voice. In the next section, we're going to look at how we respond to God's Word through the obedient act of applying the Bible to our lives.

APPLICATION

If you were to trace the origin of the word *apply* you would discover that it comes from the Latin word *applicare*, which means "to fasten to." This can refer to many things, but in the context of the practical use of the Bible, it has to do with "fastening" the truths of Scripture to our own lives. To say it another way, *application* is putting the Bible to use. As faithful students of Scripture, we're meant to seek to answer the question: *How do I use it?*

Sadly, many people tend to use Scripture in a purely subjective way; that is, they interact with the Bible only in ways that are preferential to them, thinking something like: *What does this verse mean to me?* This line of thinking places the reader in the position of authority, evaluating which truths should be put into practice. But the Word of God is meant to be approached with a spirit of humility, whereby the believer submits themselves to God and asks, "Lord, what do You want to teach me?"

In applying the Word of God, you are grasping the truth of God and bringing it to bear on your own life. Application consists of opening your soul so God's light can shine into every corner, exposing darkness and revealing the areas that need to be tended to. Hebrews 4:12 says, "For the word of God is living and active and sharper than any two-edged sword, and piercing as far as the division of soul and spirit, of both joints and marrow, and able to judge the thoughts and intentions of the heart." In other words, the Word of God is sufficient to confront us and change us. But again, we have to apply the Scripture to our hearts as we would a healing balm.

Before we apply the text, however, we first need to discover the truth that God desires to be applied. For our purposes, we must first discover the principle.

FIND THE PRINCIPLE

Wrapping your arms around a text can be challenging. Often, there is so much going on that it's hard to grasp it all. How do we apply verses and narratives? To do this, you must learn to "principlize" the Scriptures.[2] In other words, seek to find the spiritual principle being taught in the text. In order to do this, you need to interpret the text (see chapter 4) and discover what's going on in order to draw out the meaning.

The Christian refrigerator magnet industry got a huge boost when one of their product designers discovered Jeremiah 29:11. Most modern Christians have probably heard it articulated in the New International Version translation: "'For I know the plans I have for you,' declares the LORD, 'plans to prosper you and not to harm you, plans to give you hope and a future.'" At face value, this verse is incredibly encouraging and has given comfort to countless believers for years. However, this verse may in fact be one of the most misapplied verses in all of Scripture.

The prophet Jeremiah was writing to the people of Israel during the Babylonian captivity. King Nebuchadnezzar had attacked and destroyed Jerusalem, taking thousands of Jews away to Babylon, where they lived for seventy years. During their time in captivity, the people began to grow weary and lament, questioning God's promises to sustain them. However, Jeremiah delivers a series of messages, both chastising them for their previous sinfulness and giving them hope for their future deliverance. In chapter 29 of his prophecy, Jeremiah delivers his fourteenth message to Israel, in which he comforts the exiles to continue to hope in God. It is in this context where he delivers his famous line, "'For I know the plans I have for you,' declares the Lord, 'plans to prosper you and not to harm you, plans to give you hope and a future.'" Again, this verse is directed to Israelite captives living in Babylon who are awaiting their deliverance, which we read about in Jeremiah 30–33.

But how are we to apply this verse? Does this verse teach that God has plans only to prosper us and not bring us through trials? Certainly not. The general principle being taught is that God is powerful and trustworthy. He is God in whom we can hope. And while we are not sixth-century BC Babylonian exiles, as believers we identify with the people of God who place our faith in God and His promises. By studying Jeremiah 29:11, we can take comfort in the truth that, if God is faithful and able to care for His people who are held captive in Babylon, He is also faithful and able to preserve His people in the world today who are being delivered in Christ Jesus from spiritual captivity.

Learning to principlize the Scripture helps make direct application to your own life and circumstances. But the task can sometimes feel a bit overwhelming. The Bible consists of sixty-six unique books—1,189 chapters and more than 31,000 verses. How do we possibly apply all of it to our lives? It's helpful to understand that there are two different ways to apply Scripture to our lives. There are two types of outcomes that God desires for every believer.

THINGS TO KNOW

The first desired outcome consists of things that God would have us *know*. These are truths that are to be grasped. In fact, virtually every passage in the Bible teaches us something about God and His creation. Our challenge is to explore the texts and discover what we can learn. Of the infinite number of truths contained in Scripture, we can identify many different areas of study. While not exhaustive, we can learn a great deal about the following:

God

The Bible is truly the story of God given to us. Contrary to the popular sentiment that the Bible is an "instruction manual for life" or the like, the Bible was given to us so that we could come to know God and learn how we might be reconciled to Him. Therefore, the Scriptures teach us all we need to know about God. After all, Jesus prayed, "This is eternal life, that they may know You, the only true God, and Jesus Christ whom You have sent" (John 17:3). We are meant to *know God*. As J. I. Packer writes, "It is the most practical project anyone can engage in. Knowing about God is crucially important for the living of our lives."[3] What do we learn?

From the very beginning of Scripture, we see God's creative power to make the world (Gen. 1:1–2:24). We learn about the covenant promises that He makes to all humanity (Gen. 9:9–17), as well as with His people (Gen. 12:1–3; 15:1–21; 2 Sam. 7:12–16; Jer. 31:31–34). The Scriptures teach us about God's attributes (Isa. 6:3)—that God is one (Deut. 6:4–5; John 10:30) yet triune (Matt. 28:19; 2 Cor. 13:14). We learn that although God is spirit (John 4:24), He deals personally and intimately with His creation (Ex. 33:11; Acts 17:27–28). When we read the Bible, we are meant to understand that, although God very well could have kept Himself distant and disconnected from His creation, instead He chose to make Himself known through His creation (Ps. 19:1–6), His Son (John 1:14–18; Heb. 1:1–4), and His Word (Ps. 19:7–9).

Jesus Christ

When speaking to the Pharisees, Jesus rebuked them for their hard-heartedness, saying, "You search the Scriptures because you think that in them you have eternal life; it is these that testify about Me" (John 5:39). It is not the Scriptures themselves that have the power of life, but rather the Person whose Word is recorded. In other words, it is the incarnate Word who gives life (John 1:1–14). Yet wrapped up in His comments about the purpose of the Scriptures is the truth that they are ultimately about Jesus Himself. Elsewhere, in Luke 24:27, Jesus encounters two disciples on the road to Emmaus after His resurrection and instructs them "beginning with Moses and with all the prophets" (the Old Testament), explaining to them "the things concerning Himself in all the Scriptures." In short, the Bible is all about Jesus.

It is in the Scriptures that we are taught about Jesus Christ's eternality (Heb. 13:8), deity (Titus 2:13), transcendence (Col. 1:15–18), incarnation (John 1:14), virgin birth (Matt. 1:23), humanity (Heb. 2:14–18), sinlessness (Heb. 4:15), righteousness (1 Cor. 1:30–31), obedience (Rom. 5:19), humility (Phil. 2:5–8), sacrificial death (John 3:16), vicarious atonement (1 John 2:2), death (John 19:30), burial (John 19:38–42), resurrection (Luke 24:6–7), ascension (Acts 1:9), intercession (1 Tim. 2:5), and glorious future return (Rev. 19:11–16). All that we come to know and love about our Savior is taught to us in the Word of God. And the Lord desires us to know Him (John 17:3) so we might be saved by Him and conformed to His image (1 Tim. 2:4; Rom. 8:29).

The Holy Spirit

In addition to knowing God the Father and God the Son, we are also meant to know God the Spirit. While the Scriptures teach us comparatively less about the Holy Spirit, what we learn is no less paramount to our understanding of God. The Bible teaches us about the divine nature of the Spirit (Acts 5:3–4, 9) as well as His creative power (Gen. 1:2). The Spirit is given to us to regenerate us (Rom. 8:2, 6, 10–11), to indwell us (John 14:16–17), and to seal us (Eph. 1:13–14). He is "the Spirit of truth" (John 16:13; see also 14:26) who teaches and illuminates our minds to understand (1 Cor. 2:6–16) and brings comfort to us (John 16:7). And by the Word of God, the Spirit sanctifies us (1 Cor. 6:11; 1 Peter 1:2), making us more like Jesus Christ (2 Cor. 3:18). He also gives gifts to us so we may serve God and build up the body of Christ (1 Cor. 12–13; Rom. 12:3–8).

Humanity and Sin

Not only does the Bible teach us about God, it also teaches us about His creation, the capstone of which is humanity. God created humanity in His own image and likeness (Gen. 1:26–27). However, we learn that our first parents, Adam and Eve, rebelled against God (Gen. 3:1–7), bringing sin into the world (Rom. 5:12). Sin is pervasive (Rom. 3:23) and deadly (Rom. 6:23), and condemns every person to ultimate death because of its detestable nature in the sight of God (Rom. 1:18–32). However, the Bible also clearly teaches the plan and provision of God to offer salvation from sin.

Salvation

The express purpose of the coming of Jesus Christ into the world is to save people from their sins (Matt. 1:21; Mark 10:45; John 1:29; 14:6). The Old Testament foretells the arrival of the Messiah (Ps. 110; Isa. 7:14; 9:6–7; Dan. 9:24–27), and the Gospels announce His arrival to earth. We read of His sinless life and sacrificial death for sins, followed by His victorious resurrection. The epistles teach us the meaning of the coming of Christ, that we are "reconciled to God through the death of His Son" (Rom. 5:10) and saved by God's grace through our faith in Christ alone (Rom. 3:28; Gal. 2:16; Eph. 2:8–9). The Bible teaches clearly that Jesus Christ is our righteousness, salvation, and resurrection; there is no other way to God the Father than through Him.

The Church

Once a person has been saved from their sins, they are "transferred . . . to the kingdom of [God's] beloved Son" (Col. 1:13), which finds its earthly representation in the church. The Bible teaches us about the creation, nature, and function of Christ's church, whereby we are gathered together as one body (1 Cor. 12:12–27; Eph. 4:4–6), led and shepherded by pastors and teachers (Eph. 4:11; Titus 1:5–9; 1 Peter 5:1–5; Heb. 13:17), given spiritual gifts with which to serve one another (1 Cor. 14:1–40), and sent out into the world to make disciples and win the lost to Jesus Christ (Matt. 28:19–20; 1 Cor. 9:19–23).

Future Things

One area of biblical teaching that is most often misunderstood and mistaught is that of future things. The Bible teaches clearly that Jesus Christ will return one day and judge the nations (Matt. 25:31–46; Rev. 19:11–16). He will destroy sin and wickedness (Rev. 20:7–15) and create a new heaven and a new earth (Rev. 21:1–27). However, popular teaching on these events often sensationalizes them, inciting paranoia and fear. End-times literature has become big business at the expense of sound doctrine. However, the Bible teaches us that the value of knowing the future is that it gives us hope (1 Thess. 4:17–18) and motivates us to live our lives in holiness and godliness (2 Peter 3:1–13). As we watch the whole world descend into terror and madness, studious Christians learn of God's sovereign plan for the future and take comfort in His provision.

Doctrine and Theology

There are countless truths and teachings contained in the Word of God. As we read the Bible, we can begin to compile verses, passages, and themes together in our minds to formulate *doctrine*. What is doctrine? In short, it is what the whole Bible teaches on a topic.[4]

Furthermore, the study of the doctrines of God is called *theology*. Now, there are different disciplines of theology. For example, the study of the doctrine of Christ is called "Christology." The study of the doctrine on humanity is called "Anthropology" and so on. But as we dig deeper and deeper into the Scriptures, we begin to understand the mind of God and see all of life and existence through His eyes. For sure, there are many things that God wants us *to know*. However, knowledge is never meant to exist in a vacuum. It is always meant to produce in us the fruit of godliness. That's what we're going to look at next.

THINGS TO DO

The second desired outcome consists of things that God would have us *do*. These are commands to be obeyed. However, the Lord never demands blind obedience. He always gives the *why* before commanding the *what*. There is always a godly reason behind why we are to do what we do. In this section, we will look at a sample of behaviors commanded by God that we understand and apply in our study of the Bible.

Repent

The central truth of the Bible is that God is reconciling and redeeming the world through Jesus Christ. In fact, that Christ even needed to come into the world is a direct result of the fallenness of sinful humanity. With the revelation of Jesus Christ as Savior, the first response of every person who recognizes their lost condition is to *repent* of their sins. The Greek word *metanoia* literally means "to change one's mind." In the context of the Bible, it refers to a turning away from sin and turning toward God in obedience.

From the very beginning of Jesus' ministry, He preached

that all people should "Repent, for the kingdom of heaven is at hand" (Matt. 4:17; 11:20–21; Mark 1:15; Luke 13:3, 5). Furthermore, John the Baptist preached a gospel of repentance (Matt. 3:2), and so did Jesus' disciples (Mark 6:12; cf. Acts 2:38; 3:19). However, repentance is not only part of our initial turning to God for salvation. It is also an integral part of our regular Christian life, whereby we are daily confessing our sins to the Lord in order to be forgiven (1 John 1:6–2:2) and to grow in godliness. Therefore, as you study the Bible, you are meant to look for places in the text that command the confession of sins and respond accordingly.

However, there are also places in Scripture that do not explicitly tell the reader to reckon with their own sins, yet faithful application of the text mandates confession. For example, when Achan defiles the whole nation of Israel by his selfish sin in Joshua 7, he and his whole family are put to death. This is indicative (what happened to Achan), not imperative (that we should put whole families to death for sins). But we are meant to look at Achan's confession in Joshua 7:21, whereby he confesses, "I saw . . . I coveted . . . [and] took" from the Lord. Ask the questions: "Am I guilty of similar kinds of sins in my life? If I leave my sins unconfessed, will there be greater repercussions that will affect those around me?" We know that the stories in the Old Testament were not written simply for their literary value, but for our instruction and admonition (1 Cor. 10:11; see also Rom. 15:4). We ought never to waste an opportunity for self-examination. As we search the Scriptures daily, we ought to ask the Holy Spirit to convict us of sins so we may confess them to the Lord.

Believe

When the apostle John wrote his gospel in the last decade of the first century, he concluded with a purpose statement for the benefit of the reader. At the conclusion of chapter 20, John wrote, "Therefore many other signs Jesus also performed in the presence of the disciples, which are not written in this book; but these have been written *so that you may believe* that Jesus is the Christ, the Son of God; and that believing you may have life in His name" (vv. 30–31, emphasis added). Every chapter, every story, every verse of John's gospel was written explicitly to produce faith in the reader. Similarly, in Paul's letter to Titus, he opens by asserting that he was writing *"for the faith of those chosen of God* and the knowledge of the truth which is according to godliness, in the hope of eternal life" (Titus 1:1–2, emphasis added). Both John and Paul testify to the truth that the Bible was written to be read, and would thereby grow believers in their faith.

Essentially, faith is both belief and trust. Christian faith is the act of putting one's trust in the Lord God. Hebrews 11:1 calls faith "the assurance of things hoped for, the conviction of things not seen." When we read the Bible, we see the providential hand of God at work in the lives of His people, and we are meant to trust Him all the more to carry out His purpose in our own lives as well. Therefore, the truest application of studying the Bible is that our faith would grow.

The Bible is full of both examples of faithful believers as well as of deeds done by God that produce faith in His people. Hebrews 11 is the quintessential example of the faith of God's people. Often called "the Faith Chapter," Hebrews 11 presents the faith of persons in biblical history in direct response to God's providence. Spanning from Abel in Genesis to the prophets of the latter books of the Old Testament, we read of how their faith was made strong in the Lord. What does this produce in the reader? It produces action. We read in Hebrews 12:1–2:

> *Therefore, since we have so great a cloud of witnesses surrounding us, let us also lay aside every encumbrance and the sin which so easily entangles us, and let us run with endurance the race that is set before us, fixing our eyes on Jesus, the author and perfecter of faith, who for the joy set before Him endured the cross, despising the shame, and has sat down at the right hand of the throne of God.*

We are meant to study the lives and faith of those who have gone before us and apply what we learn to our own lives. As we do this, our faith in God is meant to grow. Above all, we are meant to "Trust in the LORD with all [our] heart" (Prov. 3:5), "taking up the shield of faith" (Eph. 6:16) and "[walking] by faith" (2 Cor. 5:7). After all, we read that "without faith it is impossible to please Him, for he who comes to God must believe that He is and that He is a rewarder of those who seek Him" (Heb. 11:6). In the end, we will not be able to put the truths of Scripture into practice in our own lives unless and until we put our faith solely in God through Jesus Christ. By faith, we cling to the promises of God that open the door for Him to grow us in Christlikeness.

Grow

Christians often ask, "What is God's will for my life?" It's the million-dollar, age-old question. However, it's not that difficult to figure out. While much could be discussed about the multifaceted will of God for believers, for our purposes, we need to see that God's will is that you would be sanctified—that you would *grow* in Christlikeness. The apostle Paul says it more directly: "For this is the will of God, your sanctification" (1 Thess. 4:3). The Bible teaches that God begins His sanctifying work in the life of the Christian at their salvation, and promises to bring it to completion (Phil. 1:6). The primary means by which God grows believers is through the proper and powerful administration of the Word.

There are countless verses in Scripture that encourage personal spiritual growth. Peter tells the church to "grow in the grace and knowledge of our Lord and Savior Jesus Christ" (2 Peter 3:18). The writer of Hebrews exhorted the body of Christ to "[leave] the elementary teaching about the Christ, [and] press on to maturity" (6:1). Paul exhorted the Colossian church, "Therefore as you have received Christ Jesus the Lord, so walk in Him, having been firmly rooted and now being built up in Him and established in your faith, just as you were instructed, and overflowing with gratitude" (Col. 2:6–7). But how do we apply Scripture in order to grow in the Lord?

There are numerous spiritual qualities in the Bible that are commended to the Christian believer. The New Testament features several lists of qualities (see Gal. 5:22–23; 2 Peter 1:5–8, for example), all of which serve as components of godly character. When we read the Scripture, we are meant to examine the text and challenge ourselves to grow in whatever attribute we see displayed.

Love

The last application that we will look at (which is by no means the final application) is the imperative to *love others*. If you were to boil the whole of Christianity down to one maxim, it would be that we should *love God* and *love others*. In fact, when asked which commandment was the greatest, Jesus responded, "You shall love the Lord your God with all your heart, and with all your soul, and with all your mind . . . [and] You shall love your neighbor as yourself" (Matt. 22:37, 39). While Jesus never meant that these two statements reflect every detail of the entire Christian life, He further expressed that all of Christianity is bound up within them (v. 40).

While 1 Corinthians 13:4–8 gives us the attributes of love, we understand more generally that love is the perpetual act of self-giving (John 3:16). We know that we are able to love God because He first loved us (1 John 4:19); our love for God exists in response to His perfect love. As we study the Bible, our love for God is meant to increase and abound. What about our love for others?

In John 13:34, Jesus commanded His disciples to "love one another, even as I have loved you, that you also love one another" (see also 1 John 2:7–11). In the context of John's gospel, the "one another" pertains to other Christians, but in Jesus' teaching in Matthew 22, we see that such love should be extended to anyone who is our "neighbor." More than merely expressing affection and devotion to God, we are commanded to express our love for others. The apostle Paul explains in Rom. 13:8–10 that we are to

> *owe nothing to anyone except to love one another; for he who loves his neighbor has fulfilled the law. For this, "You shall not commit adultery, You shall not murder, You shall not steal, You shall not covet," and if there is any other commandment, it is summed up in this saying, "You shall love your neighbor as yourself." Love does no wrong to a neighbor; therefore love is the fulfillment of the law.*

What does this mean? We understand that if our desire is to be obedient to God in expressing love for others, then we will act properly and virtuously in how we deal with them. For example, if we love others, we will give generously to them in their time of need (Titus 3:14). If we love others, we will speak truthfully and kindly to them (Prov. 16:24; Eph. 4:15). Beyond this, in our love for God and others, we will obey every good ordinance of man (Rom. 13:1–7; Titus 3:1–2). And while our personal situations may vary, God desires us to do the good work of prayerfully seeking His will and applying the truth of Scripture to our own lives.

There are endless points of application. The Bible has much to teach us about marriage, family, sexuality, politics, government, finance, world missions, law, and so on. The overarching key to biblical application is to place yourself at the Lord's feet and ask, "What do You want me to know and do?" Our study will likely take us to all kinds of places where we will be challenged by the Lord in every area of life. As we have seen, "The word of God is living and active and sharper than any two-edged sword, and piercing as far as the division of soul and spirit, of both joints and marrow, and able to judge the thoughts and intentions of the heart" (Heb. 4:12). In other words, your Bible is alive, energized by the power of the Holy Spirit, and it is able to change you at the heart level.

Whether we are reading examples of faithful (or unfaithful) people in narrative passages or reading the admonitions and encouragements of the epistles, we are meant to apply the imperatives of the Bible to our own lives, and ask, "Am I Christlike?" And when we're faced with the truth that we have fallen short of God's desired standard, the Holy Spirit helps us pray to Him who gives us grace generously. In the end, God desires to purify every evil desire and build in you new desires for godliness. In order to be changed by God, however, you have to eat your Bible.

Summary: If the Word of God is inspired and inerrant, it is also authoritative—it has the right to tell you how to live. The ultimate exercise entails applying the Scripture to one's own life by finding the correct spiritual principle for the situation. In the end, there are things that God wants you *to know* and things He wants you *to do*. All of it, however, is meant to draw you closer to Him, grow you as a Christian, and glorify Him as God.

Study Questions:

1. What is the *authority* of Scripture? How does it bear on your life?

2. What does it mean to *apply* the Word of God?

3. What are the two desired outcomes of studying Scripture?

4. What are some examples of things God wants you to know?

5. What are some examples of things God wants you to do?

CHAPTER SIX

EAT UP!

For forty days, Jesus wandered through the desert, hungry and tired. Pushed to His human limits, this would be the greatest test He would face until Calvary. Not only was He wrestling through hunger, thirst, and overexposure, He also endured ridicule from Satan. In Matthew 4, we read about Satan's scheme to tempt the Lord. He puts three questions to Him, the first one: "If You are the Son of God, command that these stones become bread" (v. 3). This is a direct challenge to not just His deity but also His character. Could Satan cause Jesus to stumble, and thus thwart God's plan to save humanity through Jesus' sinless sacrifice? Certainly not! But Jesus would have to give an answer. What does He do? How does He stand up against the schemes of the devil? What is His weapon of choice?

Scripture.

In verse 4, Jesus quotes Deuteronomy 8:3, rebuking Satan, "Man shall not live on bread alone, but on every word that proceeds out of the mouth of God." Jesus not only uses Scripture as a weapon, but also chooses a verse appealing to the sufficiency of God's revealed truth, even in the face of insurmountable odds. In fact, three times when Satan attacks Jesus with deceptive questions (even quoting Scripture!), the Lord fights back with the Word of God. After the third rebuke, He commands the devil to flee, and he does.

Even the King of kings recognized the power and sufficiency of the Bible for His life. He understood that, regardless of what earthly tool or provision a person possessed, it didn't hold a candle to the Word of God. Jesus upheld the truth that "Scripture cannot be broken" (John 10:35)—it cannot be divided or impugned. Further, He maintained the enduring power of Scripture, "For truly I say to you, until heaven and earth pass away, not the smallest letter or stroke shall pass from the Law until all is accomplished" (Matt. 5:18). The Lord upheld the truth, power, authority, and completeness of the Bible. And even in the deepest darkness, He affirmed that only the Word of God satisfies.

WHAT DO I DO NEXT?

Whenever you finish a book like this, it's not uncommon to feel a bit overwhelmed. *So many steps! So many things to remember!* However, rest assured that God will "equip you in every good thing to do His will, working in us that which is pleasing in His sight, through Jesus Christ" (Heb. 13:21). God will help you! Furthermore, you don't even need to knock it out of the park today. Start by taking small steps. Do the first thing.

What is the first thing?

1. Grab Your Bible

It's time to move that dusty Bible off the shelf and start unsticking some of those crisp, white pages! Keep your Bible in plain sight so that you will more easily remember to read it. I keep mine on my nightstand. My wife keeps hers on the coffee table so that it's the first thing she sees in the morning when she sits down. Do whatever works for you. However, if you don't have a good study Bible (in a translation that you can read and understand), ask your pastor or a mature believer for some help. Having a Bible that you like and feel that you can use is the first key step.

2. Decide on a Reading Plan

In this book, I'm advocating for the Seven Year Bible Plan (see chapter 3 and the appendix). Yet, however you approach your study is completely up to you. I would say that whatever you choose, be sure to stick with it. In the beginning, it may feel a bit awkward, like a new pair of shoes. But once you're into it for a bit, you'll start to grow comfortable with your plan. Trust the process. Worry about today. As Jesus said, "He who is faithful in a very little thing is faithful also in much" (Luke 16:10). Choose your plan, and purpose in your mind to stick to it.

3. Pray

As we discussed in chapter 2, prayer is essential in this process. But even before you begin, bow your head and ask God for help. I'm convinced that an earnest prayer to understand the Bible is the one prayer that God will always answer positively. Why? Because it reflects a desire to know God better, which is what He wants for all of His children. And so, don't be afraid. Resist feeling overwhelmed. Ask God for help, open the Word of God, and take the first bite.

THE SEVEN YEAR BIBLE PLAN

Earlier in the book, I described the scene that led to my discovery of the Seven Year Bible Plan. To this day, many years later, I still remember it clearly. The guilt and shame were real; the hopelessness was palpable. I've never felt more lost and alone as a Christian. But by the providence of God, the Bible that my dad gave me was sitting on my office shelf at the precise moment that it needed to be.

I recounted how *The MacArthur Study Bible* served God's purpose in my life. And it was John MacArthur's introductory preface that first taught me about his reading method. To recap: *Read through a single book of the New Testament every day for thirty days (breaking up the longer books into sections).* Again, I cannot express the feeling of relief that washed over me that afternoon. It was like an immense weight had been lifted off my back. But I had to pick a book of the Bible with which to start the plan.

Immediately, I flipped over to the table of contents in my Bible and found the shortest New Testament book I knew: Titus. The longer books still felt overwhelming, but Titus was only three chapters, forty-six verses. My thought was, *I can worry about the other sixty-five books later; right now, my whole world is Titus. I can do this.* I wasn't worried about understanding the rest of the Bible, or even the whole New Testament. I just wanted to understand Titus. I read the verses slowly and intentionally. However, I quickly realized that there was more behind the verses that I wasn't understanding. I needed help.

Up to that point, I was only vaguely familiar with John MacArthur's ministry, but I quickly found his ministry website, which was packed with thousands of sermons. As I searched through the titles, I finally stumbled onto my gold mine—twenty-seven sermons on Paul's letter to Titus. As I listened, the text opened up for me in ways I never thought possible. It was like God was removing the blinders that had been there for years. I was not only understanding the text, but loving it as well. Soon after, I discovered that many other pastors online had sermons on Titus, and I listened to every one I could find. I found myself thinking about the verses, even Googling "Ancient Crete" to learn as much as I could about the setting of the letter. For the next thirty days, I became obsessed with all-things-Titus.

DEVELOPING THE PLAN

As I noted in chapter 1, the Seven Year Bible Plan is built on the MacArthur reading plan. The basic idea is: *read each book of the New Testament thirty times over three years*. However, I soon found myself desiring to alter my approach. With my first few Bible books, I hugged pretty close to the MacArthur plan. However, after the first year, I decided to pick up my pace a bit. While I was enjoying what I was studying, I was also eager to delve into more of the New Testament. So I modified how I was reading.

One key change was that instead of logging the number of *days* in a book, I started tracking the number of "reads" through the book. By doing this, I was able to cover more ground in a shorter time, yet hopefully without sacrificing the needed time to study and meditate on the text. For example, I was able to study Galatians and James back-to-back in the same month by completing my thirty "reads" in two weeks each. I accomplished this by reading the same text both in the morning and in the evening. By logging "reads" over "days," I more than doubled the amount of content I was able to study yearly. By making this slight alteration, I was able to stay on track to finish the New Testament in three years.

For the sake of illustration, I've included my study schedule below. It's important to note that this plan is completely customizable, and you might not find my approach to be desirable for you. Nonetheless, here's how I approached the New Testament.

New Testament: Year One (Nine Sections)

In Year One, I moved a bit slower, only covering nine specific sections. My choice of books was somewhat arbitrary, although I wanted to start with books that interested me. However, I spent most of my Romans study memorizing the first ten chapters. Needless to say, Romans took me all summer long. In hindsight, I wish I had spaced out the reading more evenly over the three years.

Titus	Romans (1–5)
1 Timothy	Romans (6–10)
1 Corinthians (1–8)	Romans (11–16)
1 Corinthians (9–16)	2 Timothy
1 Peter	

New Testament: Year Two (Twenty-One Sections)

By Year Two, I had modified my method and began to study larger amounts of content. With several of the shorter books (such as 2 John, 3 John, and Jude), I doubled up and studied them simultaneously with other books.

Galatians	Colossians
James	1 John
John (1–6)	2 John
John (7–12)	3 John
John (13–21)	Philemon
2 Peter	Mark (1–5)
Jude	Mark (6–10)

Acts (1–7)	Mark (11–16)
Acts (8–13)	1 Thessalonians
Acts (14–20)	2 Thessalonians
Acts (21–28)	

New Testament: Year Three (Twenty-One Sections)

In Year Three, I knew I would be studying Revelation, so I decided to dip back into the Old Testament and study Daniel as well, to note the parallels.

Daniel (1–6)	Ephesians
Daniel (7–12)	Hebrews (1–4)
Revelation (1–5)	Hebrews (5–8)
Revelation (6–11)	Hebrews (9–13)
Revelation (12–17)	2 Corinthians (1–7)
Revelation (18–22)	2 Corinthians (8–13)
Philippians	Luke (1–6)
Matthew (1–7)	Luke (7–12)
Matthew (8–14)	Luke (13–18)
Matthew (15–21)	Luke (19–24)
Matthew (22–28)	

For the Old Testament, I crafted a different approach. While the study plan proposed in *The MacArthur Study Bible* suggested reading through the Old Testament once through yearly, I wanted to deviate in my approach. Truthfully, I wanted to replicate my New Testament study for the Old Testament. However, one glance at the sheer size of the Old

Testament made me adjust my method. I didn't want to be locked in the same reading plan for a decade, so I chose to reduce the number of "reads" from thirty down to fifteen.

Now, you will notice that my proposed "Seven Year Bible Plan" actually took me eight years! There are a few reasons for this. First, I didn't modify my reading approach until I had gotten twenty chapters into Genesis. And so, my new "fifteen reads" method didn't start until the second month. Second, after finishing Genesis, I made the painful decision to send my Bible away for rebinding, as I was using the *Ryrie Study Bible* my parents had given me when I was eight years old, and it was falling apart at the seams. Needless to say, I lost three months there. But studying 113 sections over nearly five years could feasibly have been done in four years.

Old Testament: Year Four (Twenty-Nine Sections)

While the first three years were focused primarily on the New Testament, I tried to keep my finger in the Old Testament as much as I could. I would recommend trying to keep the Old Testament fresh in your mind, reading as you are able, until you are able to transition to a more full-bodied study.

In studying the New Testament, I bounced around quite a bit, but in studying the Old Testament, I wanted to begin by following the historical books chronologically. I knew that if I bounced around, I was likely to get lost. So I made sure to work from Genesis to Esther with some measure of consistency. To break up the narrative reading, I tossed in some wisdom literature (Psalms, Proverbs, and Ecclesiastes).

Genesis (1–11)	Leviticus (1–7)
Genesis (12–20)	Leviticus (8–13)
Genesis (21–28)	Leviticus (14–19)
Genesis (29–36)	Leviticus (20–27)
Genesis (37–45)	Jonah
Genesis (46–50)	Nahum
Proverbs (1–8)	Proverbs (23–31)
Proverbs (9–15)	Numbers (1–7)
Exodus (1–8)	Numbers (8–15)
Exodus (9–15)	Numbers (16–24)
Exodus (16–22)	Numbers (25–31)
Exodus (23–28)	Numbers (32–36)
Exodus (29–34)	Ecclesiastes (1–6)
Exodus (35–40)	Ecclesiastes (7–12)
Proverbs (16–22)	

Old Testament: Year Five (Twenty-Four Sections)

The following year had me continuing in my historical reading. By this point, I was starting to get a sense of the timeline.

Deuteronomy (1–7)	Ruth
Deuteronomy (8–16)	Psalms (1–18)
Deuteronomy (17–26)	Psalms (19–34)
Deuteronomy (27–34)	1 Samuel (1–8)
Joshua (1–6)	1 Samuel (9–16)
Joshua (7–12)	1 Samuel (17–24)
Joshua (13–18)	1 Samuel (25–31)

Joshua (19–24)	2 Samuel (1–7)
Song of Solomon	2 Samuel (8–14)
Judges (1–5)	2 Samuel (15–20)
Judges (6–10)	2 Samuel (21–24)
Judges (11–15)	Judges (16–21)

Old Testament: Year Six (Twenty-Eight Sections)

My third year studying the Old Testament brought me
to a crossroads. I paused my historical study so that I could
weave in the Minor Prophets chronologically. I didn't accomplish this flawlessly, but after working through 2 Kings,
I felt confident enough that I knew when and where things
were taking place. Sprinkling in the Prophets filled out the
historical narrative and gave me a deeper appreciation of the
political and spiritual climate in Israel at the time.

1 Kings (1–7)	Habakkuk
1 Kings (8–14)	Zephaniah
1 Kings (15–22)	Haggai
2 Kings (1–8)	Zechariah (1–8)
2 Kings (9–17)	Zechariah (9–14)
2 Kings (18–25)	Nehemiah (1–7)
Amos (1–5)	Nehemiah (8–13)
Amos (6–9)	Malachi
Joel	Esther (1–5)
Micah	Esther (6–10)
Hosea (1–7)	Psalms (35–49)
Hosea (8–14)	1 Chronicles (1–8)

Obadiah	1 Chronicles (9–17)
Ezra (1–6)	Ezra (7–10)

Old Testament: Year Seven (Twenty Sections)

My initial intention was to wrap up my Old Testament study after four years, but certain missteps in my planning—rebinding my Bible and taking a few weeks off here and there—pushed me off my plan. However, I took the opportunity to work through 1 and 2 Chronicles at the end of my historical study so as to bookend the narrative. Then I moved on to the challenge of the Major Prophets. My gamble was that, with a firm grasp on Israel's biblical history, I would have the stamina to tackle Isaiah, Jeremiah, and Ezekiel. My gamble proved correct.

1 Chronicles (18–29)	Jeremiah (1–10)
2 Chronicles (1–10)	Jeremiah (11–22)
2 Chronicles (11–20)	Jeremiah (23–33)
2 Chronicles (21–28)	Jeremiah (34–47)
2 Chronicles (29–36)	Jeremiah (48–52)
Isaiah (1–12)	Lamentations
Isaiah (13–27)	Ezekiel (1–13)
Isaiah (28–39)	Ezekiel (14–22)
Isaiah (40–48)	Ezekiel (23–31)
Isaiah (49–57)	Isaiah (58–66)

Old Testament: *Year Eight (Twelve Sections)

The final year was profitable, as I finished up Ezekiel and worked through the remainder of what was missing from my Wisdom study. Once I knew that I had blown my "Seven Year" number, I relaxed and slowed down a bit. I especially wanted to enjoy my time in the Psalms. Having already studied the first fifty in previous years, ending my Bible study with the Psalms felt triumphant, especially as it hit its crescendo in Psalms 145–150.

Ezekiel (32–39)	Psalms (50–68)
Ezekiel (40–48)	Psalms (69–80)
Job (1–10)	Psalms (81–97)
Job (11–21)	Psalms (98–109)
Job (22–33)	Psalms (110–128)
Job (34–42)	Psalms (129–150)

The end of my full Bible study brought with it a tremendous sense of joy, mixed with deep feelings of reverence and awe. Over the course of seven-plus years, I accumulated a lot of biblical knowledge. But I also grew in my personal walk with the Lord. Even today, I benefit greatly from my time in the Word, which has served to propel me back in daily, longing to drink deeply from the soul-satisfying fountain of Holy Scripture.

One thing that impressed itself on me was the fact that my seven years in the Bible did not produce a sense of completion. I wasn't an "expert," nor was I "done." Rather, I had only just begun. There was more. Even now, it feels like *Step One.*

And I believe that was the Lord's intention.

DESIGNING YOUR OWN PLAN

The purpose of the Seven Year Bible Plan is to motivate whole-Bible study over long periods of time. And while it's certainly possible to follow the order I used, I suggest you create your own reading schedule. And so, to design your own plan, I would suggest a few key steps.

1. Start with the New Testament

If you've never studied the Bible before, it's wise to start in the New Testament because it focuses on the church age. In other words, you begin with Jesus Christ and the foundations of Christianity. We are new covenant Christians, and we need to know what it means to live our Christian lives in light of Christ's life, death, and resurrection. Once you have a healthy understanding of the New Testament, the Old Testament will be that much more rich and fulfilling.

2. Plan Your Reading Realistically

Spend an hour or more looking at the content of the New Testament. Be honest about your reading speed and comprehension, but challenge yourself. If you think you can read four chapters a day, write your plan to accommodate four chapters daily. But if you think you can handle only three chapters a day, build it for three; if two, then two, and so on. Alternate long and short books.

3. Decide How Long You Want to Study

While I've coined this study to be "The Seven Year Bible Plan," it doesn't necessarily have to be that for you. You may want to read each book of the Bible thirty times. You may want to read longer. You may want to read shorter. There's really no way to do this wrong, especially if you've never read or studied the Bible before. Even once through the New Testament is a win!

4. Approach the Old Testament Differently from the New Testament

While some Bible students have the stamina to be in a single book for years on end, most Christians may not. That's okay. In fact, too much focused time might actually stunt your spiritual growth if you start to become too myopic. In the end, it's important to develop a working understanding of the *whole* Old Testament and how it points to Jesus Christ. I would suggest limiting your Old Testament reading plan to fifteen reads or less so you can be finished in four or five years. Then, after you've finished, you can go back and study other sections in even greater depth.

5. Relax and Enjoy!

The worst thing you can do is allow yourself to become intimidated or feel like you're a slave to a reading plan. After all, this is *your* plan; *you* designed it! Remember, the goal is to study with a view to lifelong learning. You want to know the Bible for keeps. If you slow down, relax, and enjoy the process, you will surely get more out of your time and know the Word of God that much better.

ACKNOWLEDGMENTS

This book would have never happened without the encouragement of my wife, Jess. Right from the start, she saw it for what it could be and did not let up until the manuscript was done. Even when I began working on other projects, she would remind me, "You've got to write How to Eat Your Bible!" I've never known a more vibrant, creative, brilliant, passionate, godly person. It's an incredible kindness of God to me that she is my wife.

I'm also very grateful to Drew Dyck for sticking with me through this project. I pitched him several years ago while at the Shepherds' Conference, and he worked with me through the entire process, even through editorial, offering great insights and encouragement along the way. I'm also thankful to Kevin Emmert for his brilliant editorial work; he found the book I was trying to write. The team at Moody has been stellar: Jeremy Slager, Connor Sterchi, Grace Wise, Erik Peterson, Darren Welch, and several others who have worked on this project behind the scenes.

Eric Dodson, Dustin Benge, and Richard Mayhue read early drafts of this book and gave me helpful feedback. I approached this book with timidity due to the weightiness of the topic but was greatly blessed by the encouragement I received from them to keep working.

My deep appreciation to Tim Challies for the foreword, as well as Nancy DeMoss Wolgemuth, Abigail Dodds, Dustin Benge, Owen Strachan, Burk Parsons, Allie Beth Stuckey, and Conrad Mbewe.

Above all, human language cannot express my gratitude to the Lord Jesus Christ for His immense kindness toward me. Thank you, Lord, for plucking me out of darkness, for enveloping me in Your marvelous light, for giving me a love for Your Word, and for allowing me the great privilege of teaching others. I can taste and see that You are truly good!

NOTES

INTRODUCTION: SETTING THE TABLE

1. Matthew Barrett, *God's Word Alone: The Authority of Scripture* (Grand Rapids: Zondervan, 2016), 23.

CHAPTER 1: STARVING FOR THE WORD

1. "The State of the Bible: 6 Trends for 2014," Barna Group, April 8, 2014, https://www.barna.com/research/the-state-of-the-bible-6-trends-for-2014/.
2. Ibid.
3. "State of the Bible 2019: Trends in Engagement," Barna Group, April 18, 2019, https://www.barna.com/research/state-of-the-bible-2019/.
4. In doing research, I interacted with over two dozen articles written over the last decade, all of which expressed varying iterations of lament over the present biblical illiteracy crisis.
5. Kenneth Berding, "The Crisis of Biblical Illiteracy: And What We Can Do about It," *Biola Magazine*, Spring 2014, http://magazine.biola.edu/article/14-spring/the-crisis-of-biblical-illiteracy/.
6. Cited in Justin Taylor, "The Problem of Evangelical Biblical Illiteracy," The Gospel Coalition, January 16, 2010, https://www.thegospelcoalition.org/blogs/justin-taylor/the-problem-of-evangelical-biblical-illiteracy/.
7. According to Statistic Brain Research Institute, 46 percent of people abandon their New Year's resolutions within the first month ("New Years Resolution Statistics," Statistic Brain,

December 7, 2018, https://www.statisticbrain.com/new-years-resolution-statistics/).

8. I recognize that I am hardly the first person to suggest a paradigm shift in personal Bible study. As I was developing the Seven Year Bible Plan, I stumbled onto a helpful article full of great insights and practical tips by Jim Elliff, "My Preferred Way to Read the Bible," Christian Communicators Worldwide, December 5, 2013, https://www.ccwtoday.org/2013/12/my-preferred-way-to-read-the-bible/.

9. John MacArthur, ed., *The MacArthur Study Bible*, New King James Version (Nashville: Word Publishing, 1997), xx. While he does not in the introduction to his volume, MacArthur has elsewhere referred to James M. Gray's book *How to Master the English Bible* (Chicago: The Winona Publishing Group, 1904) as the inspiration for his approach.

10. Martin Luther, *Luther's Works: Table Talk*, vol. 54, ed. and trans. Theodore G. Tappert (Augsburg, MN: Fortress, 1967), 165.

CHAPTER 2: BEGINNING WITH PRAYER

1. Of all the wonderful books written about the doctrine of Scripture, this is one of the best: Norman L. Geisler and William E. Nix, *From God to Us: How We Got Our Bible*, revised and expanded (Chicago: Moody Publishers, 2012).

2. In his commentary on 2 Timothy, George W. Knight III, *The Pastoral Epistles*, The New International Greek Testament Commentary (Grand Rapids: Eerdmans, 1992), 445, notes that the New Testament use of the Greek word *graphē* is used for Scripture as a whole. See also Benjamin B. Warfield, *The Inspiration and Authority of the Bible* (Phillipsburg, NJ: Presbyterian and Reformed Publishing Company, 1948), 236–39.

3. John Piper, *Desiring God: Meditations of a Christian Hedonist* (Colorado Springs, CO: Multnomah, 2003), 161.

4. *The Complete Works of E. M. Bounds on Prayer* (Grand Rapids: Baker Books, 1990), 73.

CHAPTER 3: READ: WHAT DOES IT SAY?

1. Robert Saucy, *Scripture: Its Power, Authority, and Relevance* (Nashville: Word Publishing, 2001), 158.
2. R. C. Sproul, *Knowing Scripture*, rev. ed. (Downers Grove, IL: InterVarsity Press, 2009), 70–71.
3. There are seemingly endless variations of Bible reading plans. Some of the more popular ones are the Chronological Bible Reading Plan (where the Bible is reorganized according to a chronological timeline), the M'Cheyne Reading Plan (reading through the New Testament and Psalms twice, and the Old Testament once per year), and the aggressive Bible in 90 Days plan. A simple Google search will quickly reveal an endless treasure trove of options for Bible reading.
4. J. C. Ryle, *Practical Religion* (1879; repr., Faverdale North, Darlington, UK: Evangelical Press, 2001), 142–43.
5. For a helpful and accessible overview of the topic, I would recommend Wayne Grudem, Leland Ryken, C. John Collins, Vern S. Poythress, and Bruce Winter, *Translating Truth: The Case for Essentially Literal Bible Translation* (Wheaton, IL: Crossway, 2005).
6. Two helpful books on the topic of reading are Mortimer J. Adler and Charles Van Doren, *How to Read a Book: The Classic Guide to Intelligent Reading* (New York: Simon and Schuster, 1972); and Tony Reinke, *Lit!: A Christian Guide to Reading Books* (Wheaton, IL: Crossway, 2011).
7. Jonathan Edwards, "Sermons and Discourses, 1739–1742," in Owen Strachan, *Always in God's Hands: Day by Day in the Company of Jonathan Edwards* (Carol Stream, IL: Tyndale House, 2018), 193.

8. One helpful text for Bible students is J. Scott Duval and J. Daniel Hays, *Grasping God's Word: A Hands-On Approach to Reading, Interpreting, and Applying the Bible*, 2nd ed. (Grand Rapids: Zondervan, 2005). As pertaining to observing the biblical text, in chapters 2–4 of their book, they offer a lengthy discussion of what to look for.

9. Ryle, *Practical Religion*, 147.

CHAPTER 4: STUDY: WHAT DOES IT MEAN?

1. Martin Luther, *The Bondage of the Will*, trans. J. I. Packer and O. R. Johnston (Grand Rapids: Baker Academic, 1957), 71.

2. Ibid., 72.

3. Wayne Grudem, *Systematic Theology: An Introduction to Biblical Doctrine* (Grand Rapids: Zondervan, 1994), 106.

4. Gordon D. Fee and Douglas Stuart, *How to Read the Bible for All Its Worth*, 3rd ed. (Grand Rapids: Zondervan, 2003), 23.

5. R. C. Sproul, *Knowing Scripture*, rev. ed. (Downers Grove, IL: InterVarsity Press, 2009), 44.

6. Fee and Stuart, *How to Read the Bible for All Its Worth*, 29.

7. J. Scott Duvall and J. Daniel Hays, *Grasping God's Word: A Hands-On Approach to Reading, Interpreting, and Applying the Bible*, 2nd ed. (Grand Rapids: Zondervan, 2005), 21.

8. D. A. Carson, in *Matthew*, The Expositor's Bible Commentary, vol. 8 (Grand Rapids: Zondervan, 1984), 595.

9. See J. I. Packer and M. C. Tenney, eds., *Illustrated Manners and Customs of the Bible* (Nashville: Thomas Nelson, 1980), 433–35.

10. Grant Osborne, *Matthew*, Zondervan Exegetical Commentary on the New Testament (Grand Rapids: Zondervan, 2010), 75, comments on marriage and divorce in Matthew 1:18: "The key term is 'pledged in marriage'. . . which means a great deal more than the 'engagement' today. It was legally binding (a contract signed by witnesses) and could be broken only by a writ of divorce."

11. Grant Osborne, *The Hermeneutical Spiral: A Comprehensive Introduction to Biblical Interpretation*, 2nd ed. (Downers Grove, IL: IVP Academic, 2006), 28.

12. For a good sample, see Howard F. Vos, *Effective Bible Study: A Guide to Sixteen Methods* (Grand Rapids: Zondervan, 1956).

13. Robert A. Traina, *Methodical Bible Study* (1952; repr., Grand Rapids: Zondervan, 2002).

14. Richard Alan Fuhr Jr. and Andreas J. Köstenberger, *Inductive Bible Study: Observation, Interpretation, and Application through the Lenses of History, Literature, and Theology* (Nashville: B&H Academic, 2016).

15. Kay Arthur, *How to Study Your Bible: The Lasting Rewards of the Inductive Approach* (Eugene, OR: Harvest House, 1994).

CHAPTER 5: USE: HOW DO I APPLY IT?

1. Wayne Grudem, *Systematic Theology: An Introduction to Biblical Doctrine* (Grand Rapids: Zondervan, 1994), 1255.

2. John MacArthur, *How to Study the Bible* (Chicago: Moody Publishers, 2009), 133.

3. J. I. Packer, *Knowing God* (Downers Grove, IL: InterVarsity Press, 1973), 19.

4. A similar definition is given in Wayne Grudem, *Systematic Theology*, 21.

STUDY THE BIBLE WITH PROFESSORS FROM MOODY BIBLE INSTITUTE

MOODY
Publishers®

From the Word to Life®

Study the Bible with a team of 30 Moody Bible Institute professors. This in-depth, user-friendly, one-volume commentary will help you better understand and apply God's Word to all of life. Additional study helps include maps, charts, bibliographies for further reading, and a subject and Scripture index.

978-0-8024-2867-7 | also available as an eBook